WITTGENSTEIN'S
NEPHEW

WITTGENSTEIN'S NEPHEW

NEPHEW

A FRIENDSHIP

By THOMAS BERNHARD

Translated from the German by David McLintock

ALFRED A. KNOPF NEW YORK 1989

THIS IS A BORZOI BOOK
PUBLISHED BY ALFRED A. KNOPF, INC.

Copyright © 1988 by Alfred A. Knopf, Inc.

Library of Congress Cataloging-in-Publication Data

Bernhard, Thomas.   Wittgenstein's nephew.

Translation of: Wittgensteins Neffe.
1. Bernhard, Thomas—Fiction.   2. Wittgenstein, Paul, 1907–
—Fiction.   I. Title.
PT2662.E7W5813   1989   833'.914   88-45317
ISBN 0-394-56376-X

FIRST AMERICAN EDITION

*Two hundred friends will
come to my funeral
and you must make a speech
at the graveside.*

WITTGENSTEIN'S
NEPHEW

In 1967, one of the indefatigable nursing sisters in the Hermann Pavilion on the Baumgartnerhöhe placed on my bed a copy of my newly published book *Gargoyles*, which I had written a year earlier at 60 rue de la Croix in Brussels, but I had not the strength to pick it up, having just come round from a general anesthesia lasting several hours, during which the doctors had cut open my neck and removed a fist-sized tumor from my thorax. As I recall, it was at the time of the Six-Day War, and after undergoing a strenuous course of cortisone treatment, I developed a moonlike face, just as the doctors had intended. During the ward round they would comment on my moon face in their witty fashion, which made even me laugh, although they had told one another themselves that I had *only weeks, or at best months*, to live. In the Hermann Pavilion there were only seven rooms on the ground floor, accommodating thirteen or fourteen patients who had nothing to look forward to but death. They would shuffle up and down the corridor in their hospital dressing gowns, then one day disappear for ever. Once a week the great Professor Salzer, the foremost authority on pulmonary surgery, would appear in the Hermann Pavilion, always wearing white gloves and walking with an enormously imposing gait, while a bevy of nursing sisters flitted almost noiselessly around him as they escorted him, a very tall and very elegant figure, to the operating theater. This famous Professor Salzer, whom the private patients had to perform their operations, staking everything on his reputation (though I had had mine performed by the senior ward surgeon, a stocky farmer's son from the Waldviertel), was an uncle of my friend Paul, the nephew of the philosopher whose *Tractatus Logico-philosophicus* is now known to the whole of the scholarly world, to say nothing of the pseudoscholarly world. At the very time when I was lying in the Hermann Pavilion, my friend Paul was some two hundred yards away in the Ludwig Pavilion, though this, unlike the Hermann Pavilion, did not belong to the pulmonary department, and hence to the so-called Baumgartnerhöhe, but belonged to the mental institution Am Steinhof. Male Christian names are given to all the pavilions on the Wilhelminenberg, which occupies a vast area in the west of Vienna and has for decades been divided into two parts—a smaller part, reserved for chest patients and called the Baumgartnerhöhe for short (this was my territory), and a larger one, occupied by mental patients and known as Am Steinhof. It seemed grotesque that my friend Paul should be in the Ludwig Pavilion of all places. Whenever I saw Professor Salzer striding purposefully toward the operating theater, with never a glance to left or right, I could not help recalling how, time and again, my friend Paul had described his uncle alternately as a genius and a murderer, and every time I saw the Professor entering or emerging from the operating theater, I wondered whether I was seeing a genius or a murderer entering, a murderer or a genius emerging. This man's medical fame exercised a great fascination over me. Before my stay in the Hermann Pavilion, which is still devoted to lung surgery and specializes above all in lung cancer surgery, I had already seen many doctors and made a habit of *studying* these doctors, but from the moment when I first saw Professor Salzer, he put all the others in the shade. He was magnificent in every way, and this magnificence I found utterly unfathomable. His persona seemed to consist partly of the man I saw and at the same time admired, and partly of the rumors I had heard about him. According to my friend Paul, Professor Salzer had for many years been able to work miracles: patients who had apparently no chance of survival had gone on living *for decades* after he had operated on them, while others, so Paul told me time and again, had died as the result of a *sudden unforeseen change in the weather under a knife grown nervous*. Be that as it may, although Professor Salzer really was a world authority, and at the same time my friend's uncle, I did not let him operate on me, precisely because he exercised such a tremendous fascination over me and because his absolutely universal fame filled me with abject terror and made me decide, ultimately because of what I had *heard* from my friend Paul about his uncle Salzer, in favor of the worthy senior surgeon from the Waldviertel and against the great authority from Vienna's First District. During my first few weeks in the Hermann Pavilion, moreover, I had repeatedly observed that Professor Salzer's patients were the ones who did not survive their operations; his world fame was doubtless going through a bad patch, and this made me suddenly afraid of him. I therefore opted for the senior surgeon from the Waldviertel—which, as I now see, was undoubtedly a fortunate choice. But such speculations are pointless. While I myself saw Professor Salzer at least once a week, though at first only through the crack of the door, my friend Paul, who was after all his nephew, never saw him once during all the months he spent in the Ludwig Pavilion, although Professor Salzer certainly knew of his nephew's presence and it would have been the easiest thing in the world, as I thought at the time, for him to walk the few yards from the Hermann Pavilion to the Ludwig Pavilion. I do not know what reasons he had for not visiting Paul; perhaps they were weighty reasons, or perhaps he simply found it too much trouble to visit his nephew, who had frequently been a patient in the Ludwig Pavilion, whereas this was my first visit to the Hermann Pavilion. In the last twenty years of his life, my friend had to be admitted to the mental asylum Am Steinhof at least twice a year, always at short notice and always *under the most terrible circumstances*, or, if he was staying in Upper Austria when he was overtaken by one of his attacks, which grew more and more frequent as the years passed, he would be taken into the Wagner-Jauregg Hospital, near Linz. He had been born and brought up in Upper Austria, near the Traunsee, where he had right of domicile in an old farmhouse that had always belonged to the Wittgenstein family. His mental disease, which ought properly to be termed a *so-called* mental disease, manifested itself very early, when he was about thirty-five. He himself did not talk about it much, but putting together all I know about my friend, it is not difficult to form some idea of its genesis. Even as a child Paul had a predisposition to this so-called mental disease, which has never been precisely classified, having been born *mentally sick*, already suffering from the so-called mental disease that was to afflict him all his life. Until the day he died, he lived with this so-called mental disease just as naturally as others live *without* it. It furnished the most depressing evidence of the helplessness of the medical practitioners and of medical science in general. This medical helplessness of the doctors and their science led time and again to the wildest designations for Paul's so-called mental disease, though naturally never to the correct one; all these designations for my friend's so-called mental disease repeatedly proved incorrect, not to say absurd, canceling one another out in the most depressing and disgraceful fashion. The so-called psychiatric specialists gave my friend's illness first this name and then that, without having the courage to admit that there was no correct name for *this* disease, or indeed for any other, but only incorrect and misleading names; like all other doctors, they made life easy for themselves—and in the end murderously easy—by continually giving incorrect names to diseases. At every end and turn they would use the term *manic* or *depressive*, and they were always wrong. At every end and turn they would take refuge (like all doctors!) in yet another scientific term, in order to cover themselves, to protect themselves (though not the patient). Like all other doctors, those who treated Paul continually entrenched themselves behind Latin terms, which in due course they built up into an insuperable and impenetrable fortification between themselves and the patient, as their predecessors had done for centuries, solely in order to conceal their incompetence and cloak their charlatanry. From the very start of their treatment, which is known to employ the most inhuman, murderous, and deadly methods, Latin is set up as an invisible but uniquely impenetrable wall between themselves and their victims. Of all medical practitioners, psychiatrists are the most incompetent, having a closer affinity to the sex killer than to their science. All my life I have dreaded nothing so much as falling into the hands of psychiatrists, beside whom all other doctors, disastrous though they may be, are far less dangerous, for in our present-day society psychiatrists are a law unto themselves and enjoy total immunity, and after studying the methods they practiced quite unscrupulously on my friend Paul for so many years, my fear became yet more intense. Psychiatrists are the real demons of our age, going about their business with impunity and constrained by neither law nor conscience. At last I was able to get up and walk to the window, then to go into the corridor and join all the other death candidates who were still mobile in walking to the far end of the pavilion and back, and one day, when I was at last able to leave its confines, I tried to reach the Ludwig Pavilion. I had seriously overrated my strength, however, and had to give up before reaching the Ernst Pavilion. I had to sit down on a seat that was screwed into the wall in order to calm myself before I could walk back to the Hermann Pavilion unaided. When patients have lain in bed for weeks or even months and are at last able to get up, they completely overrate their strength. They simply try to do too much, and such foolishness can easily set their recovery back by several weeks; indeed many patients, by engaging in such sudden activity, have managed to bring about the death that they initially evaded through an operation. Though I am a practiced patient and have had to live with more or less serious diseases all my life —including extremely serious and so-called *incurable diseases*—I have often relapsed into a casual attitude to disease and been guilty of unpardonable stupidity. The proper way for a sick person to proceed is to start by taking just a few steps, four or five, then ten or eleven, then thirteen or fourteen, and finally twenty or thirty—not to get straight up and go straight out, which can often be fatal. But when a patient is confined to bed for months on end, he is consumed throughout these months by a longing to get out; he cannot wait for the moment when he will be able to leave the sickroom, and naturally he is not content to walk just a few paces into the corridor: he has to go out and kill himself. Many patients die through going out too soon, not through any failure of the medical art. Doctors can be blamed for many things, but however indolent they are, however lacking in conscience or even intelligence, basically all they want to do is to improve their patient's condition. But the patient has to play his part too; he must not sabotage the doctors' efforts by getting up too soon (or too late!) or by going out too soon and too far. On this occasion I had gone much too far: even

the Ernst Pavilion was too far—I should have turned back
when I got to the Franz Pavilion. But I was determined
to see my friend. I sat on the seat outside the Ernst
Pavilion, exhausted and completely out of breath, and
gazed through the trees toward the Ludwig Pavilion. Being
a chest patient and not a mental patient, I thought, I
probably wouldn't have been allowed into the Ludwig
Pavilion anyway. It was strictly forbidden for the chest
patients to leave their compound and visit that of the
mental patients, and vice versa. It is true that there were
high fences separating the two areas, but these were in
places so rusty as to be no longer secure; there were big
gaps everywhere, through which it was possible *at least
to crawl* from one area to the other, and I recall that every
day there would be mental patients in the chest patients'
area and chest patients in the mental patients' area, though
when I made my first attempt to get from the Hermann
Pavilion to the Ludwig Pavilion I did not know about
this daily traffic. Later I became familiar with the sight
of mental patients in the chest patients' area and saw with
my own eyes how they had to be rounded up by the
attendants in the evening, put into straitjackets, and driven
back into their own area with rubber truncheons, uttering
pitiful screams which pursued me into my nightly dreams.
It was of course mere curiosity that prompted the chest
patients to leave their own area and go across to see the
mental patients, hoping for something sensational that
would break up the appalling daily routine of deadly
boredom and recurrent thoughts of death. And it was no
vain hope. I was never disappointed when I left the
pulmonary department to visit the mental patients, who,

wherever they were to be seen, would be up to their curious antics. One day I may venture upon a separate account of the conditions I witnessed in the mental department. Sitting on the seat outside the Ernst Pavilion, I reflected that it would now be a whole week before I could make a *second* attempt to reach the Ludwig Pavilion, for it was clear that today I could do no more than return to the Hermann Pavilion. I sat on the seat and watched the squirrels scurrying to and fro and up and down the trees in what seemed, from where I was sitting, like an endless park. They appeared to have one consuming passion—to snatch up the paper tissues that the chest patients had dropped all over the ground and race up into the trees with them. They ran in all directions and from all directions, carrying paper tissues in their mouths, until in the gathering dusk all one could see were the paper tissues, a multitude of white dots darting hither and thither. I sat there enjoying the sight and naturally linking it with the thoughts that it seemed to conjure up automatically. It was June, and the windows of the Ernst Pavilion were open, and from these windows a rhythmical composition of rare device, a brilliant counterpoint of coughing performed by the inmates, was borne upon the evening air. Not wishing to strain the patience of the sisters, I got up and walked back to the Hermann Pavilion. Since the operation, I thought, I really can breathe better, I can breathe very well, in fact—my heart has been freed. Nonetheless, my prospects were not good, and the word *cortisone*, together with the therapy associated with it, cast a pall over my thoughts. Yet I did not necessarily spend the whole day in a mood of hopelessness. Having woken with a feeling of hopelessness, I tried to escape this feeling, and until about noon I succeeded. Then in the afternoon it returned, only to disappear again toward evening, but if I woke up during the night it was naturally back again in all its intensity. Observing that the doctors treated the patients I had seen die no differently from myself, that they exchanged the same words with them and made the same remarks, even the same jokes, I thought: The way I am going will not be much different from the way the others have gone. They died unobtrusively in the Hermann Pavilion, without screaming or crying for help, usually without a sound. In the morning their empty beds would be standing in the corridor, freshly made up for the next occupants. As we walked past, the sisters would smile, untroubled by the fact that we knew. Sometimes I thought to myself: Why do *I* want to delay the course I have to take? Why don't *I* accept it like the others? What's the point of all the effort I make on waking up, the effort of refusing to die—what's the point? Naturally I often wonder, even today, whether it would not have been better to give in, for had I done so I would assuredly have run *my* course in a very short time; I would have died within a few weeks—of that I have no doubt. But I did not die —I went on living, and I am still alive today. I regarded it as a good omen that my friend Paul was in the Ludwig Pavilion while I was in the Hermann Pavilion, though at first he did not know of my presence. However, one day he found out from our garrulous friend Irina, who visited each of us in turn. I knew that for a long time my friend had spent several weeks or months in Steinhof every year, and that *every time* he had been discharged.

This led me to believe that I too would be discharged, even though there was no comparison whatever between us. I imagined that I would spend a few more weeks in the hospital and then leave, as *he* always did. And in the end I was proved right. After four months I was able to leave the Baumgartnerhöhe; I had not died like the others, and Paul had left long before me. Yet as I walked back from the Ernst Pavilion to the Hermann Pavilion, I was still obsessed by unrelenting thoughts of death. I did not believe I would leave the Hermann Pavilion alive; I had seen and heard too much there to believe this possible, and in all I felt there was not one glimmer of hope. Nor did the dusk bring any relief, as one might imagine: it only made everything harder and almost unbearable. After being taken to task by the duty sister, who lectured me on my foolish, irresponsible, and criminal behavior, I collapsed into bed and at once fell asleep. Yet on the Baumgartnerhöhe I was never able to sleep through the night, but usually woke up after only an hour, either startled out of a dream that had taken me, like all my dreams, to the very brink of my existence or wakened by a noise in the corridor, by someone in another room who urgently needed help or was dying, or by the man in the next bed using his urine bottle. He could never use it without making a noise, even though I repeatedly told him how to do so; he usually knocked it against the iron locker next to my bed—not just once but repeatedly—and every time this happened he had to submit to an angry lecture from me about how to handle the urine bottle without waking me up. He also woke up the man on the other side of him, in the bed nearest the door (I had the one by the window). This was a policeman named Herr Immervoll, who had a passion for blackjack, a game that I learned from him and have never been able to give up, though it often drives me to the verge of insanity. And it is well known that a patient who needs sleeping pills in order to sleep at all cannot get to sleep again once he has been wakened, especially in a hospital like the one on the Baumgartnerhöhe, where all the patients were gravely sick. The man next to me was a theology student whose parents were both judges and lived in Grinzing—in the Schreiberweg, to be precise, one of the most exclusive and expensive districts of Vienna. He was an utterly spoiled character, who had never shared a room with anybody, and I was without doubt the first person to point out to him that when one is sharing a room with other people one simply has to show them some consideration. That went without saying, I added, especially if one was a theology student. But there was no way of getting through to this man, at least not at first. He had been admitted after me, also in a hopeless condition, and, like me and all the others, he had had his neck cut open and a tumor removed. The poor fellow was said to have been within a *hair's breadth* of dying during the operation, which was performed by Professor Salzer—though of course this is not to say that he would not have come *close* to dying under the hands of a different surgeon. It clearly pays to be a theology student, I thought after he moved into the room: the sisters pampered him quite disgustingly, while no less disgustingly neglecting Officer Immervoll and myself. In the morning, for instance, the night sister would bring all the presents the patients had given her during the night and put them on our theology student's locker—chocolate, wine, and all kinds of confectionery from the city, always from the choicest confectioners, of course, from Demel's and Lehmann's, and from Sluka's, the equally famous confectioners by the City Hall. They also made sure that he always got a double helping of *chaudeau*, not just the statutory single helping we were all entitled to. This frothy dessert made of eggs and wine, which was served regularly in the Hermann Pavilion and which I still love, is standard fare for the gravely sick, and all the patients in the Hermann Pavilion were gravely sick. However, I soon managed to cure our theology student of many of his antisocial habits, thereby earning the gratitude of Officer Immervoll, who was no less affected than I was by the insufferable selfishness of our fellow patient. Immervoll and I, being chronic invalids, had long since accustomed ourselves to playing the part of the considerate, unobtrusive, self-effacing patient, the only part that can make sickness endurable for any length of time; misbehavior, rebelliousness, and recalcitrance seriously weaken the system, and no chronic invalid can afford to sustain such conduct for long. One day, since our theology student was in fact quite capable of getting up and going to the toilet, I forbade him to use his urine bottle and thereby at once incurred the enmity of the sisters, who were naturally *only too pleased* to collect the theology student's bottle. I insisted on his getting up and leaving the room, because I did not see why Immervoll and I should get up and leave the room to pass water when the theology student was allowed to stay in bed to do so and thereby further pollute the already unendurable atmosphere in the room. I succeeded: the theology student, whose name I have forgotten (I think it was Walter but am no longer sure), went to the toilet, and for several days the sisters would not deign to look at me. But this did not worry me. I was only waiting for the day when I would be able to pay a surprise visit to my friend Paul, but after I had had to abandon my first attempt outside the Ernst Pavilion, this day seemed to have receded into the far distance. I lay in my bed, looking out at the unchanging view of the upper branches of a gigantic pine tree, behind which the sun rose and set for a whole week before I found the courage to leave the room. Then one day I had a visit from Irina, who had just been to see Paul. It was in Irina's apartment in the Blumenstockgasse that I had first met Paul Wittgenstein. I had dropped in during a debate on a performance of the Haffner Symphony by Schuricht and the London Philharmonic; this was right up my alley, as I too had heard Schuricht conduct the symphony the previous day at the Musikverein and felt that I had never, in the whole of my musical experience, heard a more perfect performance. All three of us—Paul, myself, and his friend Irina (who was also extremely musical and altogether extraordinarily artistic)—were of the same mind about this concert. Out of this discussion, which was naturally concerned not with fundamental questions but with crucial points that had not struck us all with equal force, my friendship with Paul grew spontaneously, as it were. I had seen him many times over a number of years, but I had never spoken to him before. It all began in the Blumenstockgasse, on the fourth floor of a house with no elevator, built around the turn of the

century. The three of us sat in an enormous room, simply
but comfortably furnished, and talked for hours, to the
point of exhaustion, about Schuricht, my favorite conductor, about the Haffner, my favorite symphony, and
about this concert, which was the foundation of our
friendship. I was immediately captivated by Paul Wittgenstein's uncompromising passion for music, a passion
that was shared by our friend Irina. He had a quite
extraordinary knowledge of music, especially of the big
orchestral works of Mozart and Schumann, as well as a
fanatical love of opera, which admittedly very soon struck
me as somewhat sinister. His love of opera was famous
throughout Vienna; it was not only feared but had something dangerously unhealthy about it, as was soon to be
demonstrated. He had a fine artistic education, by no
means confined to music, which differed from that of
others in that, for instance, he would constantly draw
comparisons, always verifiable, between works he had
heard, concerts he had attended, and different virtuosi and
orchestras he had studied. Given all these qualities, which
were absolutely authentic, as I quickly realized, I had no
difficulty in recognizing and accepting Paul Wittgenstein
as my new and quite extraordinary friend. Our friend
Irina, whose life was at least as remarkable and eventful
as Paul Wittgenstein's and who had had more marriages
and liaisons than could be counted on the fingers of two
hands, often visited us in those difficult days on the
Wilhelminenberg, turning up in a red knitted cardigan
and paying no regard to visiting hours. One day, as I
have said, she unfortunately revealed to Paul that I was
in the Hermann Pavilion and so frustrated my plan to

surprise him by suddenly appearing in the Ludwig Pavilion. It is ultimately to Irina, who is now married to a so-called musicologist and has moved out to a rural idyll in the Burgenland, that I owe my friendship with Paul. When I went into the Hermann Pavilion I had known him for two or three years, and it seemed to me no coincidence that we should both have suddenly landed on the Wilhelminenberg, *at the end of our lives*, as it were. But I did not read too much significance into this circumstance. Lying in the Hermann Pavilion, I thought to myself: I have my friend in the Ludwig Pavilion, and so I am not alone. But the truth is that even without Paul I would not have been alone during the days and weeks and months I spent on the Baumgartnerhöhe, for I had *my life support* in Vienna. I use this expression to describe the one person who has meant more to me than any other since the death of my grandfather, the woman who shares my life and to whom I have owed not just a great deal but, frankly, more or less everything, since the moment when she first appeared at my side over thirty years ago. Without her I would not be alive at all, or at any rate I would certainly not be the person I am today, so mad and so unhappy, yet at the same time happy. The initiated will understand what I mean when I use this expression to describe the person from whom I draw all my strength—for I truly have no other source of strength—and to whom I have repeatedly owed my survival. From this woman, who is wise and sensible and in every way exemplary, who has never failed me in a moment of crisis, I have learned almost everything in the past thirty years, or at least learned to understand it, and it is from her that I

still learn everything important, or at least learn to understand it. She visited me and sat on my bed nearly every
day, after laboriously making her way up to the Baumgartnerhöhe in the sweltering heat, laden with books and
newspapers, into an atmosphere that need hardly be described. She was already over seventy, yet I believe that
even today, at the age of eighty-seven, she would act no
differently. She is not the central figure in these notes
that I am writing about Paul, though even in those days
on the Wilhelminenberg, when I was isolated, shunted
aside, and written off, it was she who played the most
important role in my life and existence. The central figure
is my friend Paul, who was hospitalized with me on the
Wilhelminenberg and who also was isolated, shunted
aside, and written off. I want to see him clearly again
with the help of these notes, these scraps of memory,
which are meant to clarify and recall to mind not only
the hopeless situation of my friend but also my own
hopelessness at the time, for just as Paul's life had once
again run into an impasse, so mine too had run into an
impasse, or rather been driven into one. I am bound to
say that, like Paul, I had once more overstated and
overrated my existence, that I had exploited it to excess.
Like Paul, I had once more made demands on myself
in excess of my resources. I had made demands on everything in excess of all resources. I had behaved toward myself and everything else with the same unnatural ruthlessness that one day destroyed Paul and will one day destroy
me. For just as Paul came to grief through his unhealthy
overestimation of himself and the world, I too shall sooner
or later come to grief through my own unhealthy over-

estimation of myself and the world. Like Paul, I woke up in a hospital bed on the Wilhelminenberg, almost totally destroyed through overrating myself and the world. Paul, quite logically, woke up in the mental clinic, and I woke up in the chest clinic—he in the Ludwig Pavilion, I in the Hermann Pavilion. Just as Paul had more or less raced himself almost to death in *his* madness, I too had more or less raced myself to death in mine. Just as Paul's career had repeatedly been brought to a halt and been cut off in a mental clinic, so mine had repeatedly come to a halt and been cut off in a lung clinic. Just as Paul had again and again worked himself up to an extreme pitch of rebellion against himself and the world around him and had to be taken into a mental clinic, so I had again and again worked myself up to an extreme pitch of rebellion against myself and the world around me and had to be taken into a lung clinic. Just as Paul, at diminishing intervals, found himself and the world insupportable, as may be imagined, so I, at diminishing intervals, found myself and the world insupportable and *came to myself*, as it were, in the lung clinic, while Paul came to himself in the mental clinic. Just as the mental specialists again and again ruined Paul and then got his energies going again, so the lung specialists again and again ruined me and then got my energies going again. Paul, I am bound to say, was ultimately conditioned by madhouses, while I, it seems, have been conditioned by lung hospitals. He was educated by madmen for long periods of his life, I by lung patients; he developed in the company of madmen, I in the company of lung patients; and to develop among madmen is not so different from developing among lung patients. He learned the crucial lessons of life and existence from the madmen, whereas I learned my equally crucial lessons from the lung patients—he from mental disease, I from lung disease. It might be said that Paul succumbed to madness because one day he lost control, just as I succumbed to lung disease because I one day lost control. Paul went mad because he suddenly pitted himself against everything and lost his balance, just as one day I too lost my balance through pitting myself against everything— the only difference being that he went *mad*, whereas I, for the selfsame reason, contracted *lung disease*. But Paul was no madder than I am: I am at least as mad as he was, as he was said to be, though I have lung disease in addition to my madness. The only difference between us is that Paul allowed himself to be *utterly* dominated by his madness, whereas I have never let myself be utterly dominated by my equally serious madness; one might say that he was taken over by his madness, whereas I have always exploited mine. Paul never controlled his madness, but I have always controlled mine—which possibly means that my madness is in fact much madder than Paul's. Paul had only his madness to live on; I have my lung disease as well as my madness. I have exploited both, and one day I suddenly made them *the mainspring of my existence*. For decades Paul *lived* the part of the madman; similarly I *lived* the part of the victim of lung disease. Just as for decades Paul *played* the madman, so I *played* the victim of lung disease; and just as he *exploited* his role for his purposes, so I *exploited* my role for mine. Some people spend all their lives cherishing some great possession or some exceptional art, daring to exploit it by every possible means and making it, for as long as they live, the sole content of their lives: in the same way Paul spent all his life cherishing and exploiting his madness and using every possible means to make it the content of his life. Similarly I cherished and exploited both my lung disease and my madness, which together may be said to constitute my art. However, just as Paul became increasingly ruthless toward his madness, so I became increasingly ruthless toward my lung disease and my madness, and as our ruthlessness toward our diseases increased, so did our ruthlessness toward the world around us, which naturally became increasingly ruthless toward us. The consequence was that we ended up, at diminishing intervals, in our respective institutions—Paul in mental institutions, I in pulmonary institutions. Yet whereas our respective institutions had always been far apart, in 1967 we suddenly came together on the Wilhelminenberg, and it was there that our friendship *deepened*. Had we not ended up on the Wilhelminenberg in 1967, there might have been no such *deepening* of our friendship. Having abstained from friendship for many years, I suddenly found myself with a real friend, who understood even the maddest escapades of my far from simple and indeed quite complex mind, and was prepared to become involved in them—something that the others around me were never willing to do, because they lacked the capacity. I had only to touch on a subject, as they say, and our thoughts would develop in the right direction, and this was true not only of music, which was his specialism and mine, but of every other subject. I had never known anyone with a sharper talent for observation or a greater capacity for thought. The trouble with Paul was that he was as profligate with his intellectual fortune as he was with his financial fortune, but his intellect, unlike his finances, was inexhaustible. He never ceased to throw it out of the window, yet it never ceased to grow; the more he threw it out of the window, the more it grew. It is characteristic of people like Paul, who are at first merely crazy and are finally pronounced insane, that their intellectual fortune increases as fast as they throw it out of the window (of the mind). As they throw more and more of it out of the window, it goes on building up in the mind and naturally becomes more and more dangerous. Eventually they cannot keep up the pace, with the result that the mind can no longer endure the buildup and finally explodes. Paul's mind quite simply exploded because he could not discard his intellectual fortune fast enough. In the same way Nietzsche's mind exploded, just as all the other mad philosophical minds exploded, because they could no longer sustain the pace. Their intellectual fortune builds up at a faster and fiercer rate than they can discard it, then one day the mind explodes and they are dead. In the same way Paul's mind exploded one day and he was dead. We were alike and yet completely different. Paul, for instance, had a concern for the poor and was *also* touched by them: I too had a concern for the poor, but I was not touched by them; my mind works in such a way that I have never been able to be touched as Paul was. On one occasion Paul burst into tears at the sight of a child squatting by the Traunsee. I saw at once that it had actually been stationed there by a scheming mother in order to arouse sympathy and a bad conscience in passersby and induce them to open their wallets. Unlike Paul, I saw not only the wretched child, shamefully exploited by a greedy mother, but the mother herself, crouching in the bushes and counting a wad of bills in an appallingly businesslike manner. Paul saw only the child and its wretchedness, not the mother in the background, counting the takings. He actually cried and gave the child a hundred-schilling bill, feeling ashamed of his own existence, as it were. While I saw through *the whole scene*, Paul saw only the surface—the distress of the innocent child, not the monstrous mother in the background. This shameful exploitation of my friend's good nature was bound to remain concealed from him, while I could not fail to see it. It was typical of him that he saw only the superficial picture of the suffering child and parted with the hundred-schilling bill, while I could not help seeing through the whole scene and naturally gave the child nothing. And it was typical of our relationship that I kept my observation to myself, wishing to spare my friend, and did not tell him about the unspeakable mother counting her money behind the bushes and forcing her child to act out this charade of suffering. I left him with his superficial view of the scene; I let him give the child the hundred-schilling bill and go on blubbering, and even later I forbore to enlighten him. He often referred to this incident and recounted how he had given a hundred-schilling bill to a poor lonely child (in my presence), but I never disclosed the truth of the matter. Where the wretchedness—or ostensible wretchedness—of human beings (and humanity) was concerned, Paul never saw beneath the surface; he never saw the whole picture as I did, and the likelihood is, I fancy, that throughout his life he quite simply refused to see the whole picture, contenting himself with surface appearances for reasons of self-protection. I was never content with surface appearances—also for reasons of self-protection. That was the difference between us. In the first half of his life Paul squandered millions in the belief that he was helping the helpless (and thereby himself!), but in reality he squandered those millions on the basest and unworthiest causes—though in doing so he was of course helping himself. He continued to squander his money on those who were supposedly destitute and deserving of charity until he had none left, until he was thrown upon the mercy of his family, but their mercy was short-lived and quickly withdrawn, since mercy was to them an alien concept. Paul, for his sins, was born into one of Austria's three or four richest families, whose millions automatically multiplied year by year under the monarchy, until the proclamation of the republic led to the stagnation of the Wittgenstein fortune. Paul very soon threw away his share, more or less in the belief that by doing so he could combat poverty. The result was that for most of his life he had virtually nothing, being persuaded, like his uncle Ludwig, that it was his duty to distribute his *dirty* millions among his *spotless* fellowmen and so ensure their salvation and his own. Paul would walk through the streets with wads of hundred-schilling bills in order to distribute those dirty bills among his *spotless* fellow citizens. But the recipients were nearly always like the Traunsee child: wherever he found people to press his money on, *in order to help them* and *to make himself feel good*, they were always *Traunsee children*. When his money was gone, his relatives supported him for a very short time, acting out of a certain perverse sense of propriety, not out of generosity and not as a matter of course, because they too, it must be said, saw not just the superficial aspect of his situation but *the whole dreadful picture*. For a whole century the Wittgensteins had produced weapons and machines, until finally they produced Ludwig and Paul—the famous, epoch-making philosopher and the madman who, in Vienna at least, was equally famous and possibly more so. Paul the madman was just as philosophical as his uncle Ludwig, while Ludwig the philosopher was just as mad as his nephew Paul. Ludwig became famous through his philosophy, Paul through his madness. The one was *possibly* more philosophical, the other *possibly* more mad. But it may well be that the philosophical Wittgenstein is regarded as a philosopher merely because he set his philosophy down on paper and not his madness, and that Paul is regarded as a madman because he suppressed his philosophy instead of publishing it, and displayed only his madness. Both were quite extraordinary men with quite extraordinary brains; the one published his brain, and the other did not. I would go so far as to say that whereas the one *published* his brain, the other *put his brain into practice*. And where is the distinction between a brain that is published and constantly publishing itself and a brain that is constantly putting itself into practice? Yet if Paul had published anything, it would have been quite different from anything that Ludwig published, just as Ludwig would have practiced a form of madness quite different from Paul's. In either case, the Wittgenstein name guaranteed a certain standard, indeed the highest standard. Paul the madman unquestionably achieved a standard equal to that of Ludwig the philosopher: the one represents a high point in philosophy and the history of ideas, the other a high point in the history of madness—that is, if we insist on adhering to the conventional designations of philosophy, history, ideas, and madness, which are nothing but perverse historical concepts. In the Hermann Pavilion I was completely cut off from my friend, even though he was only two hundred yards away. I longed for nothing more intensely than to see Paul again, having for so many months been deprived of all contact with his mind and having almost suffocated among hundreds of other minds, which for the most part had nothing to offer. For let us not deceive ourselves: most of the minds we associate with are housed in heads that have little more to offer than overgrown potatoes, stuck on top of whining and tastelessly clad bodies and eking out a pathetic existence that does not even merit our pity. But the day will come when I really will visit Paul, I thought, and I made some notes about things that I intended to discuss with him, things that I had been unable to discuss with anyone for so many months. At that time I found it quite simply impossible, without Paul, to have any conversation about music or philosophy or politics or mathematics. If my musical thinking became moribund, for instance, I had only to pay Paul a visit in order to revive it. The poor fellow is locked up in the Ludwig Pavilion, I thought, possibly even in a straitjacket, when he would so much like to be at the opera. He was the most passionate operagoer Vienna has ever had, as the *cognoscenti* know. He was an opera fanatic, and even when he had become totally impoverished and finally embittered (which was inevitable), he managed to afford daily visits to the opera,

even if it meant standing through the performance. Even
when he was gravely ill he would stand through the six
hours of *Tristan* and still have the strength to shout "Bravo"
or to whistle louder than anyone before or since. He was
feared on opening nights. If he was enthusiastic he carried
the whole house with him by beginning to applaud a few
seconds before the rest. If, on the other hand, he led them
in whistling, the biggest and most expensive productions
would be flops, because *he* wanted them to be, because *he*
was in a particular mood. I can make a show a success
whenever I want, given the right conditions, he would
say, and I can also make it a total flop, given the right
conditions—and the conditions are always right—by being
the first to shout "Bravo" or the first to whistle. For
decades the Viennese did not realize that Paul was ultimately the author of their operatic triumphs, just as he
was the author of the failures at the opera house on the
Ring, failures that could be utterly disastrous if he chose.
His approval or disapproval had nothing to do with ob-
jectivity, however, but had only to do with his capricious-
ness and volatility—in other words, his madness. Many
Viennese conductors whom he could not stand fell into
his trap; he would whistle and shout at them, actually
foaming at the mouth. It was only with Karajan, whom
he detested, that he met his match. Karajan was too great
a genius to be so much as irritated by Paul. Having
observed and studied Karajan for decades, I regard him as
the most important conductor of the century, along with
Schuricht, whom I *loved*. I must say that I have *admired*
Karajan ever since I was a child, and that this admiration
is based on experience; I have respected him at least as

much as have all the musicians with whom Karajan has ever worked. Paul had a fervent hatred of Karajan, whom he habitually described as a mere charlatan, but I regarded him, from decades of observation, quite simply as the greatest musician in the world. The more famous he became, the better he became, but my friend, like the rest of the musical world, refused to see it. Ever since my childhood I have seen Karajan's genius develop and come closer and closer to perfection; I have attended almost all his rehearsals of concerts and operas in Salzburg and Vienna. The very first concerts and operas I heard were conducted by Karajan. And so I am bound to say that I had a good foundation for my musical development right from the start. The name Karajan was guaranteed to produce a fierce quarrel between Paul and me, and for as long as he lived we repeatedly quarreled about him. But my arguments could never convince Paul that Karajan was a genius, nor could his convince me that he was a charlatan. For Paul—and this in no way vitiated his philosophical system—opera was the greatest thing in the world until the day he died, while for me it was a very early passion, which by that time had been pushed rather into the background; it is an art form that I still love, but for years I have been able to live without it. When he still had the time and the means, Paul spent years traveling round the world from one opera house to another, only to announce in the end that the Vienna Opera was the greatest of them all. *The Met's no good, Covent Garden's no good, La Scala's no good.* None of them was any good compared with Vienna. *But of course*, he said, *the Vienna Opera is really good only once a year.* Only once a year—

but all the same! He could afford to visit all the famous opera houses of the world in the course of a *crazy* three-year trip, getting to know all the moderately great, really great, and positively outstanding conductors and the singers whom they courted or chastised. His head was full of opera, and as his life became progressively more dreadful—with increasing rapidity during his latter years—it too became an opera, a grand opera of course, which naturally had a tragic ending. At this moment the scene had shifted back to Steinhof and the Ludwig Pavilion, which was one of the most neglected pavilions in the whole hospital, as I was soon to discover. The *Herr Baron*, as my friend was styled by everyone, was no longer wearing his white tailcoat, tailored by Knize, as he often did at night, especially at the Eden Bar—behind my back, so to speak—even in his last years. He had once more exchanged it for a straitjacket, and instead of dining at the Sacher or the Imperial, where he was still occasionally invited by the many well-off or positively rich friends he still had—some of them aristocrats, though not all—he was once more eating from a tin bowl on the marble table in the Ludwig Pavilion. Once more he had exchanged his elegant English socks and the shoes by Magli or Rossetti or Janko for the coarse white woolen stockings and thick felt slippers that were standard issue in the Ludwig Pavilion. And he had already undergone a course of electroconvulsive therapy, which, after being discharged from Steinhof, he would describe to me in all its atrocious and inhuman detail, though not without a touch of irony and sarcasm. He was always admitted to Steinhof when the safety of those around him could no longer be ensured, when he suddenly started threatening to kill people and announcing his intention of shooting or strangling his own brothers. He would be released when he had been utterly destroyed by the megalomaniac doctors, when hardly anything stirred in him any longer and he could barely raise his head, let alone his voice. He would then retire to the Traunsee, where the family still owns a number of properties dotted about between the woods, by wonderful inlets, at the heads of glorious valleys, or on the tops of mountains—villas and farms, outbuildings and shooting lodges, where the Wittgensteins still take time off from the somewhat disagreeable routine dictated by their wealth. The Ludwig Pavilion was now Paul's *residence*. And I suddenly hesitated, wondering whether it was really wise to establish a link between the Ludwig Pavilion and the Hermann Pavilion, whether it might not do both of us more harm than good. For who knows, I thought, what state he's really in? Perhaps he's in a state that can only be harmful to me, in which case it's better not to visit him for the time being. I won't establish a link between the Hermann Pavilion and the Ludwig Pavilion. And if I did make an appearance in the Ludwig Pavilion, I thought, especially a surprise appearance, it might have a devastating effect on my friend too. I was suddenly scared of seeing him, and I thought of letting our friend Irina decide whether or not it was advisable to make contact between the Hermann Pavilion and the Ludwig Pavilion. But I immediately abandoned the idea, not wishing to involve Irina in any difficulties that might arise from whatever she decided. But at present I don't have the strength to walk across to the Ludwig Pavilion, I thought. So I abandoned the idea, since it struck me as *too absurd*. After all, there's no knowing whether Paul might not turn up *here* one day without warning. It's quite possible, I thought, since our garrulous friend Irina's told him I'm here in the Hermann Pavilion. And I was actually scared that this might happen. What if he suddenly turned up here in the Hermann Pavilion, I thought, in this strictly run ward *dedicated to death*, wearing his madman's garb, his madman's slippers, and his madman's shirt, jacket, and pants? I was afraid. I did not know how I should meet him, how I should receive him and deal with him. It'd be easier for him to visit me, I thought, than for me to visit him. If he's at all mobile, he'll be the first to make a move. Whatever the circumstances, such a visit is bound to end in calamity, I thought. I tried to repress the idea and think of something else, but of course I did not succeed. The possibility of Paul's coming to visit me became a nightmare. I felt that at any moment the door might open and Paul might come in, doing his madman act. I had visions of the attendants finding him here, putting him into a straitjacket, and driving him back to Steinhof with their rubber truncheons. I became obsessed with these dreadful visions. He's reckless enough, I told myself, to make the mistake of crawling under the fence and running into the Hermann Pavilion, then flinging himself on my bed and embracing me. When he was in a so-called critical condition he would rush up to people and hug them so tightly that they thought they would suffocate, crying his heart out as he did so. I was actually afraid that he might *suddenly* rush in and embrace me and cry his heart out. I loved him, but I did not want to be embraced by him, and I hated it when he cried his heart out to me at the age of fifty-nine or sixty. His whole body would quiver and he would stammer inarticulately, frothing at the mouth and clutching one so tightly that it became unbearable and one had to resort to violence in order to extricate oneself. I often had to fight him off, which I naturally hated doing, but there was no choice, as I would otherwise have suffocated. In his last years these hugging fits became worse, and one needed the utmost self-abnegation and almost superhuman strength to free oneself from his embrace. It had long been clear that anyone who behaved like this was dangerously sick. It was only a matter of time before he himself finally suffocated during one of his sudden attacks. *You're my only friend, the only person I have, the one and only*, he would stammer to the person he was embracing, who was at a loss to know how to calm the poor wretch, how to relieve his tension. I dreaded these embraces and feared that Paul might suddenly burst into the room. But he did not come. Every day, indeed every hour, I was afraid that he would burst in, but he did not. I learned from Irina that he was lying on his bed in the Ludwig Pavilion as if dead, refusing to eat. The methods that were used to treat him led to total debility, and when the doctors had destroyed him they left him in peace. When he was reduced to a skeleton and unable so much as to stand up unaided, they would discharge him. He would then be driven to the Traunsee, either in a car belonging to one of his brothers or alone in a taxi. Once there, he would lie low for a few days or even weeks on one of the family's estates; right up to his death he had a contractual right of domicile in a two-hundred-year-old farmhouse situated in a high valley between Altmünster and Traunkirchen, where an elderly maid with a lifelong devotion to the Wittgensteins ran a small farm to cater to the private needs of any members of the family who were on vacation in the country. At times like this his wife, Edith, would stay behind in Vienna. She knew that he would recover only if he had *nobody* around him, not even her, though she was closer to him than anyone else and he remained in love with her until his death. When he was staying by the Traunsee he would always look me up——not in the first few days, but later, when he felt able to meet people and no longer had cause to fear the ruthless stares of sensation-seekers, when he was once more in a mood to converse and philosophize. He would then turn up at Nathal, and at first, if the weather was mild, he would sit alone in the yard with his eyes closed, listening to the records I played on the first floor, from which the sound carried perfectly through the wide-open widows. *Some Mozart, please*, he would say. *Some Strauss, please. Some Beethoven, please.* I knew what records to play in order to put him into the right frame of mind. We would listen to Mozart and Beethoven together for hours, without saying a word. This was something we both loved. The day would end with a light supper prepared by me, after which I would drive him home. I shall never forget those wordless musical evenings I spent with him. It would take him about two weeks to *normalize himself*, as he put it. He would stay in the country until it began to get on his nerves and he longed to return to Vienna. Once he was there, four or five months would elapse before the first symptoms of his sickness reappeared. During the early years of our friendship he drank incessantly, and this naturally accelerated the progress of his illness. When he gave up drinking—which he did without protest—his condition at first showed an alarming deterioration and then a marked improvement. He no longer drank any alcohol. No one had enjoyed drinking as much as he had. He would drink bottles of champagne in the morning at the Sacher—but this was a mere trifle, hardly worth mentioning. At the Obenaus, a small establishment in the Weihburggasse, he would drink several liters of white wine in the course of an evening. This all took its toll. I think it was five or six years before his death when he gave up drinking. Had he not done so, he would probably have died three or four years earlier, which I think would have been an enormous pity. For it was only in the last years of his life that he developed into a real philosopher, having previously been simply a man who enjoyed the good things of life and had a bent for philosophizing, though admittedly he enjoyed life more than anyone else I have known—and this was what made him so lovable. In the Hermann Pavilion, as I lay in *fear of death*, I became clearly aware of the true value of my relationship with my friend Paul, the most valuable relationship I have ever had with another man, the only one I have been able to endure for more than the briefest period and would never have wanted to give up under any circumstances. Now, all at once, I was afraid for this man, who had suddenly become the one closest to me; I was afraid I might lose him—either *through my own death* or *through his*. During these weeks and months in the Hermann Pavilion I felt that I was close to death and that he was equally close to his in the

Ludwig Pavilion. I suddenly longed for this man, the only man I had ever been able to talk to in a way that was congenial to me, the only one with whom I could discuss and develop any topic whatever, even the most difficult. How long have I been starved of these conversations, I thought, of the chance to listen to him, to expound my own ideas and at the same time *take in other ideas*, how long is it since we talked about Webern and Schönberg and Satie, about *Tristan* and *The Magic Flute*, about *Don Giovanni* and *Il Seraglio*—how long since he sat with me in the yard at Nathal and listened to the "Rhenish" conducted by Schuricht? Only now, in the Hermann Pavilion, do I realize what I have been missing, what I have been deprived of by my renewed illness, what I have to have if I am to go on existing. I have friends, of course, the very best of friends, but none whose inventiveness and sensitivity can compare with Paul's, I thought. And from that moment I did everything I could to restore my personal contact with my unhappy friend as soon as possible. When we're both out again and *restored to health*, I told myself, I'll catch up on everything I've missed through my stay on the Baumgartnerhöhe. I had a tremendous mental need to catch up. An endless number of topics had accumulated in my mind, waiting to be discussed with him. But he was possibly still lying on his bed in a straitjacket, as our friend Irina had reported a few days earlier, staring fixedly at the ceiling, in a ward housing twenty-four similar cases, and refusing all food. I must go to him as soon as possible, I told myself. During these weeks the weather was exceedingly hot, and Immervoll in particular suffered from the heat. He had had to stop playing blackjack, and from one day to the next he became too weak to get up. His face suddenly became sunken, his nose seemed gigantic, and his protruding cheekbones gave his face a disturbingly grotesque appearance. His skin was gray and transparent, and there was hardly any flesh left on his legs. Most of the time he lay on his bed without any covers, showing no embarrassment, in the end with his legs spread wide apart. He could no longer pick up the urine bottle, and as he was constantly having to pass water, it was left to me to give it to him, because the sisters could naturally not be in our room all the time. But by now he was so clumsy that he could not aim into the bottle. Most of the time his mouth hung open, and from it ran a greenish-yellow fluid, which by midday had discolored his pillows. And suddenly he began to exude a smell that I knew well, the smell of the dying. During these days our theology student lay facing in my direction more often than in Immervoll's. He spent most of his time reading a theological work; I had the impression that he read nothing else. When his parents came over from Grinzing they sat on his bed and spent most of their time telling him that he was all they had in the world and that he must on no account leave them. *I*, however, did not have the feeling that he was on the way out. One night Immervoll was pushed out into the corridor in his bed: I had slept through his death. His bed was standing in the corridor, freshly made up, when I went to outpatients the next morning with my temperature chart, to have my weight checked. I myself was reduced to skin and bone, except for my moon face and my distended belly, which had become a horribly insensitive ball that looked as though it might burst at any moment and had a number of small fistulas on it. One day the theology student had his radio on, and hearing a broadcast of a motor race from Monza, I remembered that Paul's other consuming passion, besides music, was motor racing. In his early youth he had been a racing driver himself, and among his friends were a number of world champions in this field, which I have always found repugnant, because I can think of nothing more brainless. But my friend was like that—there were countless sides to his personality. To me it was inconceivable that the person who in my opinion had the cleverest things to say about Beethoven's string quartets and was the only one to decode the Haffner Symphony for me, revealing it to be the mathematical wonder I have thought it ever since, was also a motor racing fanatic, in whose ears the noise of cars roaring murderously round the circuit was music no less sweet. The Wittgensteins were all motor racing fanatics, and still are, and for years they used to invite the best racing drivers to stay with them in summer on their estates by the Traunsee. I recall that Paul would invite me to spend the evening and half the night at his house overlooking the Traunsee, in the company of Jackie Stewart and Graham Hill, both of them jolly fellows, as well as Jochen Rindt, who had a fatal crash at Monza shortly afterward. When Paul was over sixty he told me that he naturally saw things differently now; he saw that motor racing was brainless, as I had always told him. But Formula One clearly still had such a hold over him that it was scarcely possible to be with him without his mentioning his beloved motor racing at some point. He would find a way of bringing it into the conversation and then be unable to drop the subject, so that one instantly had to think of means of steering him away from his lifelong obsession when it suddenly took over again. He had in fact two passions, which were at the same time his two main diseases—music and motor racing. In the first half of his life it was motor racing that meant everything to him; in the second half it was music. And sailing. But how could he indulge his sporting passions now? By the time I met him they were no more than theoretical, as he had long since ceased to take any practical part in motor racing and had given up sailing. He no longer had any money of his own, and his relatives kept him on a tight budget; meanwhile, after he had for years been prone to depression, they found him a job in an insurance firm, the so-called Ringturm, where he suddenly had to earn his living, being left with no other option. As may be imagined, he did not earn much money carrying documents around and drawing up lists. But he did have a wife to support, and he had to pay for his apartment in the Stallburggasse, diagonally opposite the Spanish Riding School—and the rents in the First District are extremely high. The formerly footloose *Herr Baron* now had to turn up at the office at half-past seven in the morning, and he was spared nothing of what such an office requires. But it did not break him. Most of the time he made light of it, and when he felt inclined to describe and joke about conditions in the *city insurance company*, his imagination took flight. With these stories alone he could entertain a party all evening, saying how glad he was to be among ordinary folk at last and suddenly see what life was really like, what really went on. I think it was only because his relatives had some influence with the director that they were able to get him a job in the insurance company, for without such a connection he would not have been taken on, as no firm hires someone like him at the age of nearly sixty. Having to earn his living and support himself was a completely new experience for him, and everyone predicted that he would be a failure. But they were wrong, for until shortly before his death, when it was quite simply impossible for him to go on working for the insurance company on the Schottenring, Paul went to work punctually and left punctually, as was proper. *I'm a model employee in every way*, he often said, and I never doubted this. It was in Berlin, I believe, that he met Edith, who was his second wife—presumably before, after, or during a visit to the opera. She was a niece of the composer Giordano, who wrote *Andrea Chénier*, and most of her relatives lived in Italy, where she went every year to regenerate herself, with or without Paul (who was her third husband) but usually without him. I was extremely fond of her, and I was always glad when I came across her having coffee at the Bräunerhof. I had the most agreeable conversations with her; she not only belonged to *one of the best families*, but was a woman of more than average intelligence and charm. She was also very elegant, which for Paul Wittgenstein's wife went without saying. In what were for her unquestionably the bitterest years, when her husband's sickness was rapidly worsening and his death could be foreseen, when his attacks were becoming more and more frequent and he was beginning to spend more time in Steinhof or the Wagner-Jauregg Hospital in Linz than in Vienna or by the Traunsee, she never complained, although I know precisely under what difficult conditions she had to exist. She loved Paul, and she never deserted him, although she was separated from him most of the time, for she went on living in their little turn-of-the-century apartment in the Stallburggasse while her husband more or less vegetated in Steinhof or the Wagner-Jauregg Hospital in Linz (which had formerly been called simply the Niedernhart), wearing a straitjacket and sharing some horrible ward with others like him. His attacks did not come on suddenly, but always announced themselves weeks in advance. His hands would begin to tremble and he would be unable to finish his sentences, though he would go on talking incessantly, for hours on end, and could not be interrupted. His gait would suddenly become completely irregular: when one was walking with him he would suddenly take ten or eleven very fast steps, then three, four, or five very slow steps. He would address strangers in the street for no obvious reason, or he would order a bottle of champagne at the Sacher at ten in the morning and then leave it to become warm, without drinking it. But these are trifles. Far worse were the occasions when he ordered breakfast and then, when the waiter brought the tray to his table, seized it and hurled it against the silk-covered wall. On one occasion, as I happen to know, he got into a taxi in the Petersplatz and uttered the one word *Paris*, whereupon the driver, who knew him, actually drove him to Paris, where an aunt of Paul's who lived there had to pay the fare. Several times he took a taxi to Nathal in order to spend half an hour with me—*just to see you*, he would say—and then immediately drove back to Vienna, which is after all a distance of one hundred and thirty miles, or two hundred and sixty round trip. When he was *ripe* again, as he put it, he could not hold a glass and would lose control and burst into tears at any moment. When one met him he was always dressed in extremely elegant clothes, either bequests from friends who had died or presents from friends who were still alive. He would be sitting in the Sacher at ten in the morning in a white suit, in the Bräunerhof at half-past eleven in a gray striped suit, in the Ambassador at half-past one in a black suit, and at half-past three in the afternoon he would be back at the Sacher, wearing a fawn suit. Wherever he was walking or standing he would intone not only whole Wagner arias but often half of *Siegfried* or *Die Walküre* in his cracked voice, oblivious of his surroundings. In the street he would ask complete strangers whether they did not agree that listening to music had become unbearable now that Klemperer was gone. Most of them had never heard of Klemperer and had not the least notion about music, but that did not worry him. When the mood took him, he would deliver a lecture on Stravinsky or *Die Frau ohne Schatten* in the middle of the street and announce that he was *shortly* going to produce *Die Frau ohne Schatten* on the Traunsee, with the world's finest musicians. *Die Frau ohne Schatten* was his favorite opera, apart from those of Wagner. Indeed he repeatedly asked the most famous singers what fees they would demand for a guest appearance in *Die Frau ohne Schatten* on the Traunsee. *I'll build a floating stage*, he often said, *and the Philharmonic will play on another floating stage under the Traunstein*. Die Frau ohne Schatten *has got to be done on the Traunsee*, he said. *It has to be performed between Traunkirchen and Traunstein.*

Klemperer's death has thwarted my plans, he said. *With Böhm conducting*, Die Frau ohne Schatten *is like the morning after the night before.* On one occasion he took it into his head to go to Knize's, the best and most expensive tailors in Vienna, and have himself measured for two white tailcoats. When they were made, he informed the firm that it was absurd to deliver two white tailcoats to him when he had not even ordered *a black one.* Did they think he was crazy? In fact he was in and out of Knize's for weeks simply to arrange for alterations to the two tailcoats he had ordered. Not just for weeks but for months, the firm of Knize had been pestered by Paul's requests for alterations, and the moment the two white tailcoats were ready he denied having ordered them. *White tailcoats! Do they think I'm crazy? I wouldn't have two white tailcoats made, and certainly not by Knize's!* Armed with a wad of evidence, the firm demanded payment, and of course, as Paul had no money, the Wittgenstein family had to foot the bill. After this affair Paul naturally ended up in Steinhof again. His relatives preferred to have him there rather than at large, as they could not help thinking that he always grossly abused his freedom. They hated him, even though (indeed precisely because) he was, as I saw it, their most delightful product. It was grotesque that we should both suddenly find ourselves on the Wilhelminenberg, our hill of destiny, and in our appropriate departments, I in the pulmonary department and he in the mental department. He often tried to count on his fingers the number of times he had been in Steinhof or Niedernhart (that is to say, the Wagner-Jauregg Hospital), but he did not have enough fingers and never arrived at the right figure. During the first half of his life money was no object, because, like his uncle Ludwig, he had vast quantities of it at his disposal—inexhaustible quantities, it seemed to them—but during the second half, when he had none left, it became crucially important. During this second half of his life he went on behaving for several years as he had done in the first half, and this led to fierce quarrels with his relatives, on whom he had no legal claims whatever. His money having vanished overnight, he simply took down the paintings from his walls and sold them for a song to unscrupulous dealers in Vienna and Gmunden. Most of his valuable furniture also disappeared, in various trucks belonging to smart secondhand dealers who would give him only derisory sums for his treasures. For a Josephine commode he was paid no more than the price of a bottle of champagne, which he immediately consumed with the dealer who had *bought* the piece. In the end he repeatedly expressed a wish to go to Venice at least, in order to *have a good night's sleep at the Gritti*, but it was too late for any such wish to be realized. He gave me incredible accounts of his spells at Steinhof and the Wagner-Jauregg Hospital, which would be well worth relating, though there is no space for them here. *I was on good terms with the doctors as long as I had money, but when you run out of money they treat you like a pig*, he often said. The attendants would lock up the *Herr Baron* in one of their cages, that is to say in one of the hundreds of beds that are barred not only at the sides but on top; here he would be confined until he was broken, until he was finished—after weeks of shock therapy. The day came at last. Between lunch and visiting time, when the Her-

mann Pavilion was completely quiet, I woke up to feel
his hand on my forehead. He was standing by my bed
and asked if he could sit down. He sat on my bed and
was at first seized by a paroxysm of laughter, because it
suddenly struck him as so funny that he was with me on
the Wilhelminenberg. *You're where you belong*, he said,
and I'm where I belong. He stayed only a short while. We
agreed to pay each other frequent visits: I was to go over
to Steinhof to see him, and he was to come over from
Steinhof and visit me on the Baumgartnerhöhe—I was to
go from the Hermann Pavilion to the Ludwig Pavilion,
and he was to come from the Ludwig Pavilion to the
Hermann Pavilion. But the plan was put into effect only
once. We met halfway between the Hermann Pavilion
and the Ludwig Pavilion and sat on a bench just inside
the chest patients' territory. *Grotesque, grotesque!* he said,
and began to weep uncontrollably. For a long time his
whole body was convulsed with weeping. I walked him
back to the Ludwig Pavilion, where two attendants were
waiting for him by the door. I returned to the Hermann
Pavilion in a state of deep despondency. This meeting on
the bench, with each of us wearing his appropriate uni-
form—I that of a lung patient, he that of a Steinhof
lunatic—had the most shattering effect on me. We could
have met again, but we never did, because we did not
want to expose ourselves to a strain that was almost
unendurable. We both felt that this meeting had made
any subsequent meeting on the Wilhelminenberg impossible, and there was no need to waste a single word over
the matter. When I was finally discharged from the
Hermann Pavilion—without having died, contrary to all

predictions—and had returned to Nathal, I heard nothing from my friend for some time. I had the greatest difficulty in *normalizing* myself, and there was no question of my starting on a new work, but I did make an effort to tidy up the house, which had been somewhat neglected during my absence. Don't rush things, I told myself. It'll take time to get back to the kind of conditions that will one day make it possible to start work on a new book. When a sick person returns home after a long absence, he finds everything strange, and the process of familiarizing himself with it again, of resuming possession of everything, is long and arduous. Having lost everything, he has to rediscover it. And because a sick person is always deserted—to say anything else would be a gross lie—he must try to develop a quite superhuman energy if he wants to carry on from where he left off months before (or even years before, as I have had to do more than once). A healthy person cannot understand this and immediately becomes impatient, and by his impatience he only makes life harder for the returning invalid, though he ought to be making it easier. The healthy have never had patience with the sick, nor, of course, have the sick ever had patience with the healthy. This fact must not be forgotten. For naturally the sick make far greater demands than the healthy, who, being healthy, have no need to make such demands. The sick do not understand the healthy and the healthy do not understand the sick. This conflict often proves fatal, because ultimately the sick cannot cope with it, and the healthy naturally cannot cope with it either, with the result that they often become sick themselves. It is not easy to deal with a sick person who suddenly returns to the place from which he was wrenched by sickness, and the healthy usually lack the will to help him: they constantly play at being good Samaritans, without actually being good Samaritans or wanting to be, and because it is only a feint, it merely harms the sick person and does not benefit him. In reality, a sick person is always alone, and whatever help he gets from outside nearly always proves merely vexatious. A sick person needs the most unobtrusive help, the kind of help the healthy cannot give. Through their essentially selfish pretense of helping him they succeed only in harming him and making everything harder for him, not easier. Most of the time the sick are not helped, but merely vexed, by their helpers. When a sick person returns home, however, he cannot afford any vexation. Should he point out that he is being vexed rather than helped, he will at once be rebuffed by those who are ostensibly helping him; he will be accused of arrogance and boundless selfishness when in fact he is only resorting to the ultimate self-defense. When a sick person returns home, the healthy world receives him with ostensible kindness, ostensible helpfulness, ostensible self-sacrifice, but its kindness, helpfulness, and self-sacrifice, when put to the test, turn out to be a sham, and one does well to forgo them. But of course there is nothing more difficult than to recognize genuine kindness, genuine helpfulness, and genuine self-sacrifice; there is nothing harder than to distinguish between the *genuine article* and the *sham*. For a long time we may believe that we are dealing with the genuine article, only to discover that we have been taken in by a sham. The hypocrisy practiced by the healthy toward the sick is extremely common.

Basically the healthy want no more to do with the sick, and they are put out if a sick person—one who is gravely sick—suddenly reasserts his claim to health. The healthy always make it particularly difficult for the sick to regain their health, or at least to normalize themselves, to improve their state of health. A healthy person, if he is honest, wants nothing to do with the sick; he does not wish to be reminded of sickness and thereby, inevitably, of death. He wants to stay with his own kind and is basically intolerant of the sick. It has always been made difficult for me to return from the world of the sick to the world of the healthy. While a person is sick, the healthy shun him and cast him off, in obedience to their instinct for self-preservation. Then suddenly this person who has been shed and has meanwhile ceased to matter reappears and claims his rights. Naturally he is at once given to understand that basically he has no rights. As the healthy see it, the sick have forfeited whatever rights they once had (here I am speaking of the gravely sick, those with chronic diseases, like Paul Wittgenstein and myself). Their sickness has robbed them of their rights and thrown them upon the charity of the healthy. When a sick person, having ceded the place that he once occupied by right, suddenly demands its restitution, the healthy regard this as an act of monstrous presumption. A sick person who returns home always feels like an intruder in an area where he no longer has any business to be. It is a well-known pattern the world over: a sick person goes away, and once he is gone the healthy move in and take over the place he formerly occupied, yet instead of dying, as he was meant to do, he suddenly returns, wishing to resume and repossess his former place. The healthy are incensed, since the reappearance of this person whom they had already written off forces them back into their previous confines, and this is the last thing they want. The sick person needs the most superhuman strength if he is to resume and repossess his former place. On the other hand, it is well known that the gravely sick, once they return home, set about the *reappropriation* of their rights with the utmost ruthlessness. Sometimes they even have the strength to displace the healthy, to drive them out and even to kill them. But this very rarely happens: the normal situation is the one I have already described, in which the sick person returns home, expecting nothing but gentleness and consideration, only to meet with brutal hypocrisy, which, with a kind of clairvoyance, he is at once able to see through. A gravely sick person who returns home must be treated with gentleness and consideration. But this is difficult, and therefore rare. The healthy immediately make him feel he is an outsider and no longer one of them, and while pretending that this is not so, they do all in their power to repulse him. I met with none of these difficulties, since I returned to a completely empty house, and Paul, who was discharged before me, was fortunate in being able to return to Edith. I have hardly ever known a more helpful person than my friend's wife; she surrounded him with loving care until one day, about six months before his death, she suffered a stroke that left her partially paralyzed. She had a long spell of hospitalization, and then for some months she would be seen in the city center, but of course she was no longer the Edith she had once been. She had lost much of her self-confidence

and insisted on doing her shopping in the immediate
vicinity of their apartment, and since cooking was now
such an effort, she went for lunch to the Grabenhotel in
the Dorotheergasse, where the food has always been cheap
but was still of excellent quality, as it no longer is. After
the death of the two proprietors of the hotel, who also
owned the Regina and the Royal and both died of Parkin-
son's disease, the food in all three establishments became
inedible, and it is a long time since I last visited any of
them—which is a great pity, as the Grabenhotel is the
most pleasant place to sit. One day Edith died, leaving
my friend Paul completely alone. He went rapidly down-
hill. At times he seemed like his former self, but death
was *written on his face*, as they say, and he knew it. He
had absolutely nothing more to lose in the world. Once
or twice he tried to recuperate in the Salzkammergut, but
to no avail. While Edith was alive he had left her alone
most of the time in their apartment above the Bräunerhof,
but now that she was dead he could no longer exist without
her. He seemed *lost*, and there was no longer any way of
helping him. I and various other friends often took him
out for a drink—to take him out of himself, as they say—
but without success. Once or twice he himself invited me
and my friends to the Sacher and ordered champagne, as
in the old days, but this only deepened his depression. In
their last years together, when he was not in Steinhof or
in the Wagner-Jauregg Hospital (Wagner-Jauregg, after
whom this psychiatric hospital was named, had been a
relative of his), he and Edith often went to Traunkirchen.
Now he went there alone, but the effect was devastating.
Even at a distance one could see that he was desperate,

rushing this way and that and finding nothing to cling to.
In his own quarters, up on the hill between Altmünster
and Traunkirchen, in a house that belonged to a brother
(who spent most of the year in Switzerland) and only
partly to Paul, it was so cold, all the year round, that as
soon as one entered one felt that before long one would
freeze to death. The high walls were damp right up to
the ceiling. On them hung four hideous paintings, spotted
with mold, from the Klimt period, and beside these was
one by Klimt himself, who, like other famous painters
of his day, was commissioned to paint the portraits of the
arms-producing Wittgensteins, since it was the fashion
among the *nouveaux riches* at the turn of the century to
have their portraits painted, under the pretext of patron-
izing the arts. The Wittgensteins, like the rest of their
kind, had basically no interest in art, but were keen to
patronize it. In a corner of the room stood a Bösendorfer
grand, on which, as may be imagined, all the virtuosi of
their time had played. The main reason for the freezing
conditions was that the huge tiled stove in the ground-
floor room had been out of order for decades, so that for
decades it had been impossible to heat the house. The
stove therefore acted as a refrigerator. Whenever I saw
Paul and Edith sitting by it, they were wrapped in fur
jackets. In the Salzkammergut the houses have to be
heated until June, and then again from mid-August on-
ward. It is a cold and unfriendly region, perversely described as a *summer resort*, and for anyone with a sensitive
constitution it is lethal. Everyone there suffers from
rheumatic disorders; all the old people are bent and de-
formed, and one has to be very strong to survive. The

Salzkammergut is marvelous for a few days but annihi-
lating if one stays there for any length of time. Paul loved
the Salzkammergut, having spent his childhood there, but
it increasingly depressed him. He went there from Vienna
in the hope that his health would improve, but it only
worsened. He found the Salzkammergut more and more
oppressive, both physically and mentally. I went for walks
with him near Altmünster, but they did him no good.
We were still able to have *ideal* conversations, but after
Edith's death everything suddenly became hopeless, or at
least radically changed. It was as though everything had
been *destroyed*. It was an effort for him to laugh. Apart
from the death of his beloved wife, he had reached the
age when everything becomes doubly difficult. In the
room where we sat, the air was so damp and stale that I
thought I would suffocate, even though outside it was
sunny. I realized why he and his wife hardly ever stayed
at the house, preferring the little boardinghouse down by
the main road, where they did not have to do everything
for themselves. After the age of sixty nobody likes doing
everything for himself, and Edith was nearly eighty when
she died. I recall that he went sailing again on the
Traunsee, with my brother and me. It was an absurd
thing to do. Though gravely ill, Paul was in his element
and as enthusiastic as ever, while I cursed this sailing trip
and the high waves on the lake. My brother tried to get
Paul to go for another outing on the lake, but it was no
use: he was far too weak. Although this trip made him
happy while we were *on the lake*, it depressed him as
soon as we were back on shore, since he knew it was his
last. He kept on saying, *It's the last time*, and this became

a refrain. If I had friends staying with me he would go for walks with us. He was not keen to do so, but was prepared to join us. I do not care for walks either, and have been a reluctant walker all my life. I have always disliked walking, but I am prepared to go for walks with friends, and this makes them think I am a keen walker, for there is an amazing *theatricality* about the way I walk. I am certainly not a keen walker, nor am I a nature lover or a nature expert. But when I am with friends I walk in such a way as to convince them I am a keen walker, a nature lover, and a nature expert. I know nothing about nature. I hate nature, because it is killing me. I live in the country only because the doctors have told me that I must live *in the country* if I want to survive—for no other reason. In fact I love everything except nature, which I find sinister; I have become familiar with the malignity and implacability of nature through the way it has dealt with my own body and soul, and being unable to contemplate the beauties of nature without at the same time contemplating its malignity and implacability, I fear it and avoid it whenever I can. The truth is that I am a city dweller who can at best tolerate nature. It is only with reluctance that I live in the country, which on the whole I find hostile. And naturally Paul too was a city dweller through and through, who, like me, was soon exhausted when surrounded by nature. On one occasion I had to have a copy of the *Neue Zürcher Zeitung* because I wanted to read an article about Mozart's *Zaïde* that was due to appear in it. Believing that I could obtain a copy in Salzburg, I drove the fifty miles to this so-called *world-famous* festival city, with Paul and a woman friend of ours, in her car. But the *Neue Zürcher Zeitung* was not to be had in Salzburg. Then I had the idea of getting a copy in Bad Reichenhall, and so we drove to this *world-famous* spa. But the *Neue Zürcher Zeitung* was not to be had there either, and so we drove back to Nathal, somewhat disappointed. Just outside Nathal, Paul suddenly proposed that we drive to Bad Hall, another *world-famous* spa, where we would be sure to get the *Neue Zürcher Zeitung* and so be able to read the article on *Zaïde*. So we actually drove the fifty miles from Nathal to Bad Hall. But the *Neue Zürcher Zeitung* was not to be had there either. Since it was *just a stone's throw*, a mere twelve miles, from Bad Hall to Steyr, we drove to Steyr, but the *Neue Zürcher Zeitung* was not to be had there either. We then tried our luck in Wels, but the *Neue Zürcher Zeitung* was not to be had in Wels either. In all, we had driven two hundred and twenty miles just to get the *Neue Zürcher Zeitung*, and all to no avail. As may be imagined, we were completely exhausted, and so we went to a restaurant in Wels to relax and have something to eat, the hunt for the *Neue Zürcher Zeitung* having brought us to the limit of our physical endurance. It occurs to me now, as I recall this episode, that Paul and I were very much alike. Had we not been totally exhausted, we would certainly have driven on to Linz and Passau, perhaps even to Regensburg and Munich, and in the end we would have thought nothing of simply driving to Zurich to buy the *Neue Zürcher Zeitung*, for in Zurich, I fancy, we would have been certain to get a copy. Since we failed to get the *Neue Zürcher Zeitung* that day, because it is not taken in any of the places we visited, even during the summer months,

I can only describe these places as miserable shitspots, which thoroughly deserve this description, if not an even shittier one. I also realized at the time that no one with intellectual pretensions could possibly exist in a place where the *Neue Zürcher Zeitung* is unobtainable. To think that I can get the *Neue Zürcher Zeitung* all the year round in Spain and Portugal and Morocco, even in the smallest town boasting only one drafty hotel—but not in this country! And the fact that we could not get the *Neue Zürcher Zeitung* in all these supposedly famous places, including Salzburg, aroused in us anger and indignation toward this small-minded, backward country with its backwoods mentality and its sickening *folie de grandeur*. We should live only in a place where we can at least get the *Neue Zürcher Zeitung*, I said, and Paul wholeheartedly agreed. But then the only place left to us in Austria is Vienna, for in all the other towns where the *Neue Zürcher Zeitung* is allegedly available it cannot in fact be obtained. At any rate not every day, and not when one wants it, when one simply has to have it. It occurs to me that I never got to see the article on *Zaïde*. I forgot about it ages ago, and naturally I survived without it. But at the time I believed that I just had to have it. And Paul supported me in my craving; indeed it was actually he who urged me on through half of Austria and as far as Bavaria in my quest for the article and the *Neue Zürcher Zeitung*— and, what is more, in an open car, with the inevitable consequence that the three of us had colds for a week and Paul had to spend a long time in bed. I spent hours walking with him along the Traun, starting from the Kohlwehr, upriver from Steyermühl, just over a mile

from my house. The riverbank still exists, but thanks to
the rapacity of its present owner, who, as I know, has
parceled it all off, it will soon cease to be the unique park
it is at present, stretching for eight miles down to the
lake. We walked along by the river, which the famous
Herr Ritz classified as having the best trout fishing in the
world, and in the pleasant half-shade, with the wonderfully
cool air coming up from the river, we suddenly began to
have the kind of conversations we had had before, but
naturally Paul's interests had developed in the meantime,
so that he was concerned no longer with grand opera but
with chamber music. Even in spirit he had dissociated
himself from the big opera houses. He no longer talked
about Chaliapin and Gobbi, about Di Stefano and Sim-
ionato, but about the art of Thibaud and Casals, about
the Juilliard Quartet and the Amadeus Quartet, and about
his beloved Trio di Trieste, about the differing techniques
of Arturo Benedetti Michelangeli and Pollini, of Rubin-
stein and Arrau or Horowitz, etc. He now bore what they
call the mark of death. I had known him for over ten
years, and in all these years he had been gravely ill,
bearing the mark of death. On the Wilhelminenberg,
sitting on the seat where the only words he uttered were
Grotesque, grotesque, we had set a permanent seal on our
friendship, as they say, without speaking a word. It was
difficult now to imagine that thirteen or fourteen years
earlier he had been in love with an American soprano
who played the Queen of the Night and Zerbinetta in
nearly all the world's great opera houses and that he had
followed her around the world, though in the end he had
to give her up and be content to dream about her. It was

inconceivable that at that time, not so very long ago, he had attended the most famous motor races in Europe and taken part in them himself, and that he had been one of the finest yachtsmen—inconceivable that for decades he had spent most of his nights in Europe's most famous bars and never gone to bed before three or four in the morning, that he had even been a professional dancing partner at one time, in defiance of all the principles and precepts of the Wittgensteins—that this was the man who had once frequented all the best hotels of old-time Europe and fashionable Europe. And it was inconceivable now that this was the man who had shouted or whistled when the Viennese opera reached its most splendid heights or its most abysmal depths. During the last sad years of his life everything he had lived through became inconceivable. Sitting with me by the wall in the yard at Nathal as the sun went down, he tried to work out how often he had been in Paris, how often in London and Rome, how many thousands of bottles of champagne he had drunk, how many women he had seduced, how many books he had read. This seemingly superficial existence had not been led by a superficial person. Quite the contrary. There was hardly an occasion when he had any difficulty in following one's ideas and developing them further. In fact *he* often shamed me by putting me right in precisely those fields which were properly mine and in which I was convinced I was at home. Very often I would think: *He's* the philosopher, not me, *he's* the mathematician, not me, *he's* the expert, not me. And in the field of music there was hardly anything that he could not immediately call to mind and make the starting point for at least an interesting musical debate. Moreover, he was a quite extraordinary coordinator as far as this particular intellectual or artistic discipline was concerned. On the other hand, he was by no means a voluble talker, let alone a blatherer, in a world that seems to be full of voluble talkers and blatherers. One day, probably impressed by one of his extraordinary accounts of his life, I suggested that he set down all the things he had told me, with so much philosophical stiffening, so to speak, rather than let it perish with time. But it took me years to persuade him to consider writing down these universally interesting experiences of his. To pursue this purpose, he said, he would have to quit his present surroundings and get out of the clutches of his stupid relatives, who were opposed to everything pertaining to the mind and art, and naturally he would have to get away from all the houses the Wittgensteins had built as bastions against the mind and art. Then, having bought a stack of paper, he would have to take a room somewhere where he could not be disturbed. And so he booked himself into a little hotel outside Traunkirchen. But he gave up after one attempt. Later, eighteen months before his death, he suddenly engaged a secretary so that he could dictate to her an account of his curious existence. But because he was kept so short of money during his last years, this attempt too was a more or less miserable failure. He had promised this secretary a *fortune*, as I heard both from her and from Paul, telling her that she would become enormously rich if she would let him dictate his curious existence to her, for he was convinced that his *parochial memoirs*, as he called them, would be a huge success worldwide. Nevertheless, he did manage to write ten or fifteen pages. Basically, he was probably not wrong in believing they would be a *huge success* (this was his own phrase): such a book might well have been a huge success. It would certainly have been what is called a *unique* work, but he was not the man to isolate himself for upwards of a year in pursuit of such an aim. All the same, it is a pity that not more such fragments by him are extant. Where business was concerned the Wittgensteins always thought in millions, and it was quite natural that Paul, their black sheep, should also think in millions when it came to publishing his memoirs. I'll write about three hundred pages, he said, and there'll be no problem about finding a publisher. He believed he could find the right one for his manuscript. It was to be a thoroughly philosophical account of his life, *not just a rigmarole*, as he put it. In fact I often saw him carrying around a sheaf of papers containing a good deal of text, and he may well have written more than has survived. He may have destroyed large parts of his manuscript during one of his attacks, in an access of extreme self-criticism: from what I know of him this would have been quite natural. Yet it is also possible that his writings somehow got lost or were spirited away, as they say, by someone who did not care for art and philosophy. For it is hard to imagine that he spent two years or more on the same ten or eleven pages, carrying them around with him in Vienna or by the Traunsee. When he was back *in form*, he would tell his *circle of friends* that he was far superior to me as a writer, and that while he admired me and regarded me as his model, both as a writer and as a philosopher, he had long since surpassed me and my ideas and made himself independent. When his book was published, he said, the literary world would not be able to get over its astonishment. Finally, toward the end of his life, when he was under extreme pressure as a writer and obviously found that verse came more easily to him than prose, he wrote a number of poems—with the left hand, as it were— which were really amusing, full of madness and wit. Just before being readmitted to one of his madhouses, he would read out the longest of them to anyone willing to listen. There is a tape recording of this poem, which centers upon himself and Goethe's Faust; listening to it, one is highly amused and at the same time deeply disturbed. I could recount not just hundreds, but thousands of Paul's anecdotes in which he is the central figure; they are famous in the so-called *upper reaches* of Viennese society, to which he belonged and which, as everybody knows, have lived on such anecdotes for centuries; but I will refrain from doing so. He was a restless character who always lived on his nerves and was perpetually out of control. He was a brooder, endlessly philosophizing and endlessly accusing. He was also an incredibly well trained observer, and over the years he developed his gift for observation to a fine art. He was the most ruthless observer and constantly found occasion to accuse. Nothing escaped his accusing tongue. Those who came under his scrutiny survived only a very short time before being savaged; once they had drawn *suspicion* upon themselves and become guilty of some *crime*, or at least of some *misdemeanor*, he would lambaste them with the same words that I myself employ when I am roused to indignation, when I am forced to defend myself and take action against the insolence of the world in order not to be put down and annihilated by it. In the summer we had our regular places on the terrace of the Sacher, where we spent most of our time in accusations. Whatever came within range became a target for fresh accusations. We would sit on the terrace for hours over a cup of coffee, accusing the whole world, root and branch. Having taken our places on the terrace of the Sacher, we would switch on our well-tried accusation mechanism behind what Paul called *the arse of the opera*. (If one sits on the terrace in front of the Sacher and looks straight ahead, one has a rear view of the opera house.) He took pleasure in such formulations as *the arse of the opera*, even though this one denoted the rear elevation of the house on the Ring which he loved more than anything else in the world and from which he had for so many decades drawn virtually everything requisite to his existence. We would sit on the terrace for hours and watch the passersby. I still know of no greater pleasure—in Vienna—than to sit on the terrace of the Sacher in summer, watching the world go by. Indeed, I know no greater pleasure than observing people, and to observe them while sitting in front of the Sacher is a particular delight that Paul and I often shared. The *Herr Baron* and I had discovered a corner of the terrace that was specially suited to our purposes, where we could see everything we wanted without being seen by anyone. Walking with him through the center of the city, I was amazed to discover how many people he knew and how many of them were actually relatives of his. He seldom spoke of his family, and when he did it was only to say that basically he wanted nothing to do with it and that his family, for its part, wanted nothing to do with him. Now and then he would mention his *Jewish* grandmother, who had committed suicide by throwing herself out of the window of her house in the Neuer Markt, and his aunt Irmina, who had been a so-called *Reich peasants' leader* in the Nazi period and whom I knew from several visits to her farmhouse on the hill overlooking the Traunsee. When he said *my brothers* he meant *my tormentors*. The only person he spoke of with affection was a sister who lived in Salzburg. He had always felt threatened and shunned by his family, which he described as a family that was inimical to the mind and art and choking on its millions. Yet it was this family that had produced Ludwig and Paul—and then rejected them at the most convenient moment. Sitting with my friend by the wall of the yard at Nathal, I reflected on the course his life had taken over the past seventy years. He had had as much wealth and protection as anyone could possibly have. He had grown up in the inexhaustible Austria of the monarchy and had naturally been educated at the famous Theresianum, but then he had quite consciously struck out on a course of his own which was opposed to the family tradition, turning his back on what were, to a superficial view, the Wittgenstein values—wealth and property *and* protection—in order to lead a so-called intellectual existence and thereby save himself. One might say that he made an early getaway, as his uncle Ludwig had done years before, abandoning everything that had, after all, made them both possible, and transforming himself, like his uncle Ludwig before him, into what the family regarded as a *shameless character*. Ludwig transformed himself into a shameless philosopher, Paul into a shameless madman. Moreover, it is far from certain that a philosopher can qualify as such only by writing down and publishing his philosophy, as Ludwig did: he remains a philosopher even if he does not publish his philosophizings, even if he writes nothing and publishes nothing. Publishing merely clarifies and causes a stir through what it clarifies, which cannot be clarified or cause a stir unless it is published. Ludwig published his philosophy, Paul did not: Ludwig was the born publisher (of his philosophy), Paul the born nonpublisher (of his philosophy). Yet in their own ways both were great, original, revolutionary thinkers, whose thinking was always exciting and of whom their age can be proud—and not only their own age. It is naturally a pity that Paul left us no written, printed, or published evidence of his philosophy, such as we have from his uncle Ludwig, both in our hands and in our heads. But it is nonsense to compare Ludwig and Paul. I never talked to Paul about Ludwig, let alone about his philosophy. Only occasionally, and somewhat to my surprise, Paul would say, *Of course you know my uncle Ludwig.* That was all. We never once talked about the *Tractatus.* On one occasion, however, Paul said that his uncle Ludwig was *the maddest member of the family. After all, to be a multimillionaire and a village schoolteacher is a bit perverse, don't you think?* I still know nothing of the real relations between Paul and his uncle Ludwig, nor did I ever inquire about them. I do not even know whether they ever saw each other. All I know is that Paul flew to the defense of his uncle Ludwig whenever the family attacked and made fun of him. I gathered that Wittgenstein the philosopher was a source of embarrassment to them as long as he lived. Ludwig Wittgenstein, like Paul Wittgenstein, was always the fool who had greatness conferred on him by foreigners—and foreigners always have a flair for oddity. They would shake their heads and find it droll that *the world had been taken in by the fool of the family,* that *the useless one had suddenly acquired fame in England and become the great intellectual.* The Wittgensteins, in their arrogance, quite simply rejected their philosopher and accorded him not the slightest respect, and they are still punishing him with their contempt, seeing in him, as they saw in Paul, nothing but a traitor. They *discarded* him as they discarded Paul. Having been ashamed of Paul as long as he lived, they are ashamed of Ludwig to this day. This is the truth, and not even Ludwig's considerable fame has been able to stifle the family's habitual contempt for its philosopher, in a country where Ludwig Wittgenstein ultimately counts for nothing and is scarcely known even today. Not even Sigmund Freud has been properly recognized or acknowledged by the Viennese; this is a fact, and the reason for it is that the Viennese are far too perfidious. And Wittgenstein has fared no differently. When Paul referred to *my uncle Ludwig* it was in a tone of the greatest respect, but he never chose to elaborate, preferring to content himself with the mere mention of his uncle. I was never clear about his relations with this uncle who achieved greatness in England. My relations with Paul, which began in our friend Irina's apartment in the Blumenstockgasse, were naturally difficult. It was the kind of friendship that has to be daily renewed and re-won, and in the course of time this proved exceedingly strenuous. Our friendship constantly shifted between high points and low points, relying for its continuance on repeated *proofs of friendship*. I recall, for instance, the important part that Paul played on the occasion when I was awarded the Grillparzer Prize—how he alone, apart from my companion, saw through the contrived absurdity of the award ceremony and hit upon the proper designation for such a grotesque: *a piece of genuine Austrian perfidy*. I recall that I bought a new suit for the occasion, believing that I could not appear at the Academy of Sciences unless I wore a suit. Accompanied by my companion, I went to an outfitters in the Kohlmarkt and chose one that seemed appropriate. Having tried it on, I decided to go on wearing it. It was gray-black, and I believed that in this gray-black suit I would be better able to play my part than in my old suit. On the morning of the ceremony I still regarded the conferment of the prize as a great occasion. It was the hundredth anniversary of Grillparzer's death, and to be singled out for the award of the Grillparzer Prize on the hundredth anniversary of the poet's death seemed to me a signal distinction. I'm now being honored by the Austrians, I thought, by my fellow countrymen, who up to now have done nothing but kick me, and, what's more, by the award of the Grillparzer Prize. I really thought I had reached some peak of achievement. It is possible that my hands were trembling that morning, and that I was somewhat light-headed. That the Austrians, having previously scorned or ignored me, should be giving me their highest award struck me as a kind of overdue compensation. It was not without a certain pride that I emerged from the clothing store into the Kohlmarkt, wearing my new suit, and walked over to the Academy of Sciences. Never in my life have I walked along the Kohlmarkt and the Graben and past the Gutenberg monument with such a sense of elation. Yet although I felt *elated*, I cannot say that I felt comfortable in my new suit. It is always a mistake to buy clothes under supervision—in company, so to speak—and I had made the mistake *yet again*: the new suit was too tight. All the same, I probably look quite good in my new suit, I thought as I arrived in front of the Academy of Sciences with my companion and Paul. If one disregards the money that goes with them, there is nothing in the world more intolerable than award ceremonies. I had already discovered this in Germany. They do nothing to enhance one's standing, as I had believed before I received my first prize, but actually lower it, in the most embarrassing fashion. Only the thought of the money enabled me to endure these ceremonies; this was my sole motive for visiting various ancient city halls and tasteless assembly rooms—until the age of forty. I submitted to the indignity of these award ceremonies—until the age of forty. I let them piss on me in all these city halls and assembly rooms, for to award someone a prize is no different from pissing on him. And to receive a prize is no different from allowing oneself to be pissed on, because one is being paid for it. I have always felt that being awarded a prize was not an honor but the greatest indignity imaginable. For a prize is always awarded by incompetents who want to piss on the recipient. And they have a *perfect right* to do so, because he is base and despicable enough to receive it. Only in extremities, when one's life and existence are threatened—and only until the age of forty—is one jus-

tified in receiving any prize or distinction, with or without
an accompanying sum of money. When I received my
prizes I did not have the excuse that I was suffering
extreme hardship or that my life and existence were
threatened; hence by receiving them I made myself not
only low and contemptible but positively vile, in the truest
sense of the word. On the way to receive the Grillparzer
Prize, however, I believed that this time it was different.
The prize carried no emolument. The Academy of Sciences
meant something, I told myself, and its prize meant
something. And as the three of us arrived in front of the
Academy I believed that this prize was exceptional, since
it was called the Grillparzer Prize and was being conferred
by the Academy of Sciences. And as I walked across to
the Academy of Sciences I actually thought it likely that
I would be received *outside* the building, as seemed appropriate, and *with the appropriate respect*. But there was
no one there to receive me. I waited in the entrance hall
for a good quarter of an hour with my friends, but no one
recognized me, let alone received me, even though my
friends and I spent the whole time looking around. No
one took the slightest notice of us as hordes of people
streamed in and took their seats in the crowded assembly
room. In the end I decided that we should simply follow
the crowd. I decided to take my place in the middle of
the room, where there were still a few empty seats, and
went and sat there with my friends. By the time we had
taken our seats the room was full, and even the minister
had taken her place in the first row in front of the dais.
The Vienna Philharmonic was nervously tuning up, and
the president of the Academy of Sciences, a man by the

name of Hunger, was running excitedly to and fro on the dais, while only I and my friends knew what was holding up the ceremony. Several members of the Academy were running back and forth on the dais, looking for the central figure in the proceedings. Even the minister turned and looked around the room in all directions. Suddenly one of the gentlemen on the dais caught sight of me sitting in the middle of the room and, whispering something in the president's ear, left the dais and began to make his way toward me. It was not easy for him to pass along the row of seats, which were all occupied, to where I was sitting. Everyone in the row had to stand up. They did so only reluctantly, and I saw the malignant glances that were directed at me. It occurred to me that it had been a monstrous idea of mine to sit in the middle of the room, causing the utmost difficulty to the gentleman who was trying to reach me (and who of course was a member of the Academy). Obviously nobody here has recognized you, I thought at once, except for this gentleman. By the time he reached my place all eyes were fixed on me—and what reproachful, penetrating looks they gave me! An academy that gives me a prize and doesn't know me from Adam, and then sends me reproachful, penetrating looks because I haven't made myself known, deserves to be treated with even greater contempt, I thought. Finally the gentleman pointed out to me that my proper place was not where I was sitting but in the front row beside the minister, so would I please go to the front row and sit next to her. I did not obey, because the request was made in a rather disagreeable and arrogant tone, and with such a sickening assurance of victory that, to preserve my self-respect, I *had* to refuse to accompany him toward the dais. *Herr Hunger himself* should come, I said; it was for *the president of the Academy himself*, not just anybody, to invite me to approach the dais. It would have given me the greatest pleasure to get up and leave the Academy of Sciences with my friends, without receiving the prize. But I stayed where I was. I was locked in my own cage. There was no way out. I had made a cage for myself out of the Academy of Sciences. Finally the president of the Academy came down and accompanied me toward the dais. No sooner had I sat down next to the minister than my friend Paul, unable to contain himself any longer, burst into a peal of laughter that shook the whole room and continued until the Philharmonic began to play. A few speeches were made about Grillparzer and a few words said about me. Altogether the talking went on for an hour; as is customary on such occasions, there was far too much talking, and naturally it was all nonsense. The minister slept through the speeches, snoring audibly, and woke up only when the Philharmonic struck up again. When the ceremony was over, as many people as possible crowded round the minister and President Hunger. No one took any further notice of me. Before my friends and I left the assembly room, I heard the minister cry out: *Where's the budding poet?* By this time I had had enough and left the Academy of Sciences as fast as I could. No money *and* being pissed on—that was intolerable. I ran out into the street, more or less dragging my friends after me, and I can still hear Paul saying to me as we left: *You've let yourself be abused! These people have pissed on you!* It's true, I thought, they really have pissed on you. They've pissed on you again, as always. But you allowed yourself to be pissed on, I thought, and, what's more, in the Viennese Academy of Sciences. Before going to the Sacher with my friends to digest this whole perverse prize-giving procedure over a boiled fillet of beef, I went back to the outfitter's in the Kohlmarkt where I had bought my new suit before the ceremony. I told them that it was too tight and I wanted a new one. I said this with such insolent emphasis that the staff did not demur, but at once set about finding me a new suit. I took one or two off the rack and tried them on, finally choosing the most comfortable. I paid a small additional sum and kept the suit on. When I was back in the street, it struck me that before long somebody else would be running around in Vienna in the suit I had worn for the conferment of the Grillparzer Prize at the Academy of Sciences. The thought amused me. I had equally clear evidence of Paul's strength of character on another occasion, when I received the State Prize for Literature (long before the Grillparzer Prize). This ended in what the newspapers called a *scandal*. The encomium delivered by the minister in the audience chamber of the ministry was utter nonsense, because he merely read out from a sheet of paper what had been written down for him by one of his officials charged with literary affairs. He said, for instance, that I had written a novel about the *south seas*, which of course I had not. And although I have been an Austrian all my life, the minister stated that I was Dutch. He also stated that I *specialized in adventure novels*, though this was news to me. More than once during his encomium he said that I was a foreigner, *a visitor to Austria*. By this stage I was no longer annoyed

by the idiocies he read out. I knew that this imbecile
from Styria could not be blamed, because before becoming
a minister he had been secretary to the Chamber of
Agriculture in Graz, with special responsibility for stock
breeding. Stupidity was written all over his face, as it is
over the faces of all ministers without exception. It was
distasteful, but not annoying, and I was able to endure
his speech without difficulty. It then fell to me to say a
few words, by way of thanks for the prize, as it were.
Just before the ceremony, in great haste and with the
greatest reluctance, I had jotted down a few sentences,
amounting to a small philosophical digression, the upshot
of which was that man was a wretched creature and death
a certainty. After I had delivered my speech, which lasted
altogether no more than three minutes, the minister, who
had understood nothing of what I had said, indignantly
jumped up from his seat and shook his fist in my face.
Snorting with rage, he called me a *curr* in front of the
whole assembly and then left the chamber, slamming the
glass door behind him with such force that it shattered
into a thousand fragments. Everybody present jumped up
and watched in astonishment as the minister stormed out.
For a moment complete silence reigned, as they say. And
then the strangest thing happened: the whole assembly,
whom I can describe only as an opportunistic rabble,
rushed after the minister, though not without shouting
curses and brandishing their fists at me as they went. I
clearly remember the clenched fist that Herr Henz, the
president of the Art Senate, brandished at me, and all the
other marks of respect I was shown at that moment, as
the whole assembly, consisting of a few hundred kept

artists, most of them writers—colleagues of mine, one might say—together with their hangers-on, raced through the shattered glass door in pursuit of the minister. I will refrain from mentioning names, as I have no wish to appear in court over such a ludicrous matter, but they were the best known, most celebrated, and most respected names in Austrian letters. They all raced out of the audience chamber and down the stairs after the minister, leaving me standing there with my companion. Like a leper. None of them stayed behind with us; they all rushed out, past the buffet that had been prepared for them, and followed the minister down the stairs—all except Paul. He was the only one who stayed with me and my companion, horrified, yet at the same time amused, by the incident. Later, when they could safely do so, a few of those who had at first disappeared slunk back and joined me in the audience chamber. This little group finally got around to discussing where to go for a meal in order to choke down the whole ridiculous episode. Years later Paul and I would go through the names of those who had raced after this brainless Styrian politician in their unscrupulous subservience to the state and its ministers, and we knew why each of them had done so. The following day the Austrian newspapers carried reports of how *Bernhard the nest fouler* had insulted the minister, when in fact the opposite was the case: the minister Piffl-Perčević had insulted the writer Thomas Bernhard. However, the event drew fitting comment abroad, where people do not have to rely on the Austrian ministries and their involvement in artistic subventions. *Accepting a prize is in itself an act of perversity,* my friend Paul told me at the time, *but accepting a state prize is the greatest.* Visiting our *musical* friend Irina in the Blumenstockgasse had become one of our favorite habits, and it was nothing short of a disaster when one day she moved to the country, to a remote village in Lower Austria that could be reached only after a two-hour drive, as it did not even have a rail connection. We could not imagine what a city dweller like Irina hoped to find in the country. Year in, year out, she had gone to a concert or the opera or the theater every evening, yet now she suddenly took a lease on a one-story farmhouse, half of which was used as a pigsty, as Paul and I discovered to our horror, and where not only did it rain in but damp rose from floor to ceiling, there being no cellarage. Suddenly there she was, sitting with her musicologist, who for years had written for Austrian newspapers and periodicals, leaning against an American cast-iron stove, eating her own home-baked farm bread, wearing shabby old clothes, extolling the country life and inveighing against the city, while I had to hold my nose against the stench from the pigsty. The musicologist no longer wrote articles on Webern and Berg, Hauer and Stockhausen, but spent his time chopping wood outside the window or clearing out the blocked cesspit. Irina talked no longer about the Sixth or the Seventh but only about the smoked pork she hung in the chimney with her own hands, no longer about Klemperer and Schwarzkopf but about the neighbor's tractor, which woke her at five in the morning to the accompaniment of the dawn chorus. At first we thought it would not be long before Irina and her musicologist spouse lost their fascination for husbandry and returned to music, but we were deceiving ourselves. There was soon no more talk of music—it was as though it had never existed. We drove out to see her and were given home-baked bread and home-made soup, home-grown radishes and home-grown tomatoes. We felt we had been let down and led up the garden path. In a few months Irina, until recently a sophisticated city dweller with a passion for Vienna, had transformed herself into a stolid provincial farmer's wife who spent her time hanging smoked pork in her chimney and growing her own vegetables. To us this seemed a gross self-degradation, and we could not help being disgusted, so we soon stopped driving out to see her, and she actually vanished from our horizon. We were obliged to seek a new venue for our conversations and discussions, but found none: there was no substitute for the Blumenstockgasse. Thrown upon our own resources without Irina, we were suddenly deprived of all musical inspiration as we sat in the Sacher or the Bräunerhof—or the Ambassador, which also had an ideal corner for the likes of us, where we could see everything without being seen and where our conversations were not instantly stifled as soon as they got under way. Not caring for walks, we would meet somewhere and at once set off for the Sacher or one of the other coffeehouses that suited our purposes. Seated in *our* corner at the Sacher, we would at once find a victim for our speculations. Seeing some other guest, either an Austrian or a foreigner, self-consciously eating his cake or a portion of Prague ham stuffed with the ever-popular horseradish cream, or drinking coffee as he recovered from a strenuous sightseeing tour of the city—and therefore consuming his cake too hastily or gulping down his coffee too greedily—we would launch into denunciations of the mindless gluttony that had generally been on the increase in recent decades. From some German woman, sitting there in her tasteless fur coat and spooning up the whipped cream with gusto, we would derive our distaste for all the Germans in Vienna. Some Dutchman sitting by the window in a loud yellow pullover, endlessly picking pellets of snot from his nose and believing himself unobserved, would at once inspire a blanket condemnation of everything pertaining to the Netherlands, which we suddenly felt we had detested all our lives. If we saw nobody we knew, we had to make do with strangers, but if an acquaintance appeared on the scene, he would become the focus of observations that were precisely tailored to their object and could keep us amused literally for hours. To dispel our boredom we would exploit these observations in the service of what we fancied were rather more exalted topics, as starting points for discussions of quite different subjects that we ventured to regard as entirely philosophical. Thus some quite ordinary person, sitting there drinking his coffee, would often launch us into a discussion of Schopenhauer, or a lady sitting with her naughty grandchild under the portrait of an archduke and working her way through great slices of apple strudel might set us talking for hours about the court jesters of Velázquez in the Prado. If an umbrella fell to the ground, it put us in mind not only of Chamberlain, as one might imagine, but of President Roosevelt, or a passerby with a little Pekingese might conjure up the extraordinarily lavish life-style of the Indian maharajas. And so on. When I am in the country, bereft of mental stimulus, my thinking atrophies, because my whole mind atrophies, but nothing so calamitous ever happens to me in the city. As Paul once put it, people who leave the city for the country and want to keep up their intellectual standards have to be equipped with tremendous potential, with incredible mental resources, yet sooner or later even they are prone to stagnation and atrophy, and by the time they become aware of this process it is usually too late, and they inevitably come to a miserable end without being able to help themselves. Hence, throughout the years of my friendship with Paul I accustomed myself to the lifesaving rhythm of constantly switching between the city and the country, a rhythm that I intend to maintain for the rest of my life—going to Vienna at least every other week, and at least every other week to the country. For in the country the mind is drained just as fast as it is recharged in Vienna—faster, in fact, since the country always treats the mind more cruelly than the city ever can. The country robs a thinking person of everything and gives him virtually nothing, whereas the city is perpetually giving. One has simply to see this, and of course feel it, but very few either see it or feel it, with the result that most people are sentimentally drawn to the country, where in no time they are inevitably sucked dry, deflated, and destroyed. The mind cannot develop in the country; it can develop only in the city, yet today everyone flees from the city to the country because people are basically too indolent to use their minds, on which the city makes the greatest demands, and so they choose to perish surrounded by nature, admiring it without knowing it, instead of seizing upon all the benefits the city has to offer, which have increased and multiplied quite miraculously over the years, and never more so than in recent years. I know how *deadly* the country is, and whenever possible I flee from it to some big city—no matter what it is called or how ugly it is—which always does me a hundred times more good than the country. I have always cursed my unhealthy lungs, which prevent me from spending all my time in the city, which is what I would most like to do. But it is senseless to go on agonizing over something that cannot be changed and has not been worth talking about for years—something I must refrain from talking about. It occurs to me how lucky my friend Paul was to have good lungs and not to have to live in the country merely to survive. He could afford what I regard as the greatest boon—to spend all his time in the city—something that I could never afford if I wanted to go on living. Although he had not drunk alcohol for years, his favorite nightly resort, even in the last year of his life, was the *Eden Bar*, for naturally he could not bear to stay at home after Edith died. Only now did I learn why he had never invited me up to his apartment, even though we had met hundreds of times at the Bräunerhof, which was in the same building. This apartment consisted of one quite large room and a small adjacent room that served as both kitchen and bathroom. Only a few months before his death he took me to this *apartment*, climbing laboriously up the stairs, which were probably even more taxing for me than they were for him, since for years I have hardly been able to climb stairs and am out of breath after three or four flights. The elevator being out of order and the stairway in almost complete darkness, we groped our way up the stairs, urging each other on by our panting.

The apartment itself was *not much to write home about*, he said after we had entered, but the *location* was *superb*. One could not be more central, he said, and the location was what mattered most to him, aside from the fact that he could afford this apartment but not a bigger one. *Naturally that was very depressing for Edith*, he said, pointing to the half-open door to the kitchen-cum-bath, behind which were heaps of dirty linen and crockery, and a great pile of groceries that had been kept too long to be usable. The last refuge of a failure, I thought. We sat down on a sofa covered in black-and-green velvet to get our breath back before we could think of doing anything more than make embarrassed remarks about the cramped space, the dirt, the darkness, and the ideal location of the apartment. The sofa was from his childhood, he said, from his parents' home; it was his favorite piece of furniture. I can no longer say what we talked about as we sat on the sofa, but I soon got up and took my leave, while my friend remained sitting hopelessly on his black-and-green sofa. I suddenly could not stand being with him any longer. I kept thinking that I was no longer sitting with a living person, but sitting with one who had long been dead, and so I made my escape. Before I was out of the apartment he began to weep, his hands pressed between his knees, because he suddenly saw once more that it was all over, but I was determined not to turn back. I went down the stairs and into the open air as fast as I could. I ran along the Stallburggasse and the Dorotheergasse, then across the Stephansplatz to the Wollzeile, where I was at last able to slacken my pace. I sat down on a bench in the City Park and ordered myself to breathe regularly as I tried to escape from my situation; it was a terrible situation, in which I kept feeling that I was about to suffocate. Sitting on the bench in the City Park, I thought that I had perhaps seen my friend for the last time, for I could not believe that such a debilitated body, which had hardly a spark of life left in it, since all will to live had gone, could survive for more than a few more days. What shattered me most was that this man was suddenly so alone—a man like him, who was born and brought up to be what they call a man of society and had finally grown old. I thought of how I had met this man, who really had been my friend, who had so often brought so much happiness into my existence, which, though not actually unhappy, was a burden most of the time, who had acquainted me with so much that was at first quite foreign to me, pointing me in ways I had not known before, opening doors that had previously been closed, and who brought me back to my true self at the crucial moment when I might easily have gone to pieces in the country. For before I met my friend there had been a period when I was prey to a morbid melancholy, if not depression, when I really believed I was lost, when for years I did no proper work but spent most of my days in a state of total apathy and often came close to putting an end to my life by my own hand. For years I had taken refuge in a terrible suicidal brooding, which deadened my mind and made everything unendurable, above all myself—brooding on the utter futility all around me, into which I had been plunged by my general weakness, but above all my weakness of character. For a long time I could not imagine being *able* to go on living, or even existing. I was no longer capable of seizing upon any purpose in life that would have given me control over myself. Every morning on waking I was inevitably caught up in this mechanism of suicidal brooding, and I remained in its grip throughout the day. And I was deserted by everyone because *I* had deserted everyone—that is the truth—because I no longer wanted anyone. I no longer wanted anything, but I was too much of a coward to make an end of it all. It was probably at the height of my despair—a word that I am not ashamed to use, as I no longer intend to deceive myself or gloss over anything, since nothing can be glossed over in a society and a world that perpetually seeks to gloss over everything in the most sickening manner— that Paul appeared on the scene at Irina's apartment in the Blumenstockgasse. He was so different from anyone I had ever met, so new to my experience (and with a name, moreover, that for decades I had revered like no other), that I at once felt him to be my deliverer. Sitting on the park bench, I suddenly saw it all clearly again, and I was not ashamed of the pathos I succumbed to, of the fine words that I allowed to flow into me for the very first time; they suddenly made me feel tremendously good, and I made no attempt to tone them down. I let them all descend on me like a refreshing rain. And today it seems to me that we can count on the fingers of one hand all the people who have really meant anything to us in the course of our lives, and very often this one hand protests at our perversity in believing that we need a whole hand in order to count them, for to be honest we could probably make do without a single finger. There are times, however, when life is endurable, and at such times we occasionally manage to count three or four people to whom in the long run we owe something, and not just something but a great deal—people who have meant everything and been everything to us at certain critical moments or certain critical periods of our lives. Yet we know that as we get older we have to employ ever subtler means in order to produce such endurable conditions, resorting to every possible and impossible trick the mind can devise, though it may be stretched to the limits of its tolerance even without having to perform such unnatural feats. Yet at the same time we should not forget that the few people in question are all dead, that they died long ago, for bitter experience naturally inhibits us from including the living in our calculation—those who are still with us, perhaps even at our side—unless we want to risk being totally, embarrassingly, and ludicrously wrong, and hence making fools of ourselves, above all in our own eyes. I would certainly have no such inhibition with regard to Ludwig Wittgenstein's nephew Paul. On the contrary, this man, to whom I was linked for years, until his death, by every possible passion and disease, and by the ideas that were constantly engendered by those passions and diseases, was one of the people from whom I derived so much benefit throughout those years, who did so much to enhance my existence—in a way that accorded with my aptitudes, abilities, and needs—and very often made its continuance possible. This is now clear to me beyond all question, two years after his death, as I face the January cold and the January emptiness of my house. Now that I have no living person left, I tell myself, I will face the January cold and the January emptiness with the help of the dead, and of all these dead there is none closer to me, at this time and at this moment, than my friend Paul. I stress the word *my*, for what is set down in these notes is the picture that *I* have of my friend Paul Wittgenstein, no other. We gradually discovered that there were countless things about us and within us that united us, yet at the same time there were so many contrasts between us that our friendship soon ran into difficulties, into ever greater difficulties, and ultimately into the greatest difficulties. Yet I now see that throughout these years my whole being was in some elemental way controlled by this friendship, consciously or unconsciously—controlled by a friendship which neither of us found easy and to which we had to devote the most strenuous effort if it was to remain useful and profitable to us both, while at the same time taking the utmost care never to lose sight of its fragility. Sitting on the park bench, I recalled that at the Sacher he always preferred to sit in the right-hand lounge, because he found the chairs there more comfortable but above all because he judged the paintings on the walls to be better executed, while I naturally preferred to sit in the left-hand lounge, because of the foreign newspapers, especially the English and French newspapers, that were always available there and because of the more wholesome air. When we went to the Sacher, therefore, we would sit sometimes in the right-hand and sometimes in the left-hand lounge. When I was in Vienna (and in those years I spent most of my time in Vienna) the Sacher was our favorite resort, since it was ideally suited to our speculations; it therefore went without saying that we would meet there or, if for some reason the Sacher was out of the question, at the Ambassador. I have known the Sacher for nearly thirty years, since the time when I used to sit there nearly every day with friends belonging to the circle of the brilliant composer Lampersberg, who was also as mad as he was brilliant. At this time, around 1957, I had just completed my studies, and it was the most difficult period of my life. These friends introduced me to the refined world of the Sacher, Vienna's premier coffeehouse—not, I am thankful to say, to one that was frequented by the literary folk, whom I have basically always found repugnant, but to one frequented by their victims. At the Sacher I could get all the newspapers, which I have always had to have since the age of twenty-two or twenty-three, and could spend hours studying them in one of the comfortable corners of the left-hand lounge without being disturbed. I can still see myself sitting there for whole mornings, scanning the pages of *Le Monde* or *The Times* and never having my enjoyment interrupted for a moment; as far as I recall I was never disturbed at the Sacher. At a literary coffeehouse I could never have devoted myself to the newspapers for a whole morning without interruption; before so much as half an hour had passed I would have been disturbed by some writer *making his entrance*, accompanied by his retinue. I always found such company distasteful because it deflected me from my real intentions, rudely impeding what I considered essential and never facilitating it, as I would have wished. The literary coffeehouses have a foul atmosphere, irritating to the nerves and deadening to the mind. I have never learned anything new there but only been annoyed and irritated and pointlessly depressed. At the Sacher I was never irritated or depressed, or even annoyed, and very often I was actually able to work—in my own fashion, of course, not in the fashion of those who work in the literary coffeehouses. At the Bräunerhof, above which my friend had lived for years before we met, I am still put off by the foul air and the poor lighting, which is kept down to a minimum—doubtless from perverse considerations of economy—and in which I have never been able to read a single line without effort. I also dislike the seating, which is inevitably damaging to the spinal column, however briefly one sits there—to say nothing of the pungent smell that emanates from the kitchen and very soon gets into one's clothes. Yet at the same time the Bräunerhof has great merits, though these do not suffice for my peculiar purposes. They consist of the extreme attentiveness of the waiters and the unfailing courtesy of the proprietor, which is neither exaggerated nor perfunctory. But at the Bräunerhof a dreadful twilight reigns all day long—a boon to young couples or old invalids but not to someone like myself, who wishes to concentrate on studying books and newspapers. I attach the utmost importance to reading books and newspapers every morning, and in the course of my intellectual life I have specialized in reading English and French newspapers, having found the German press unbearable ever since I first began to read. What is the *Frankfurter Allgemeine*, for instance, compared with *The Times*, I have often asked myself, what is the *Süddeutsche Zeitung* beside *Le Monde*? The answer is that the Germans are just not English and certainly not French. From my early youth I have regarded the ability to read English and French books and newspapers as the greatest advantage I possess. What would my world be like, I often wonder, if I had to rely on the German papers, which are for the most part little more than garbage sheets—to say nothing of the Austrian newspapers, which are not newspapers at all but mass-circulation issues of unusable toilet paper? At the Bräunerhof one's thoughts are immediately stifled by cigarette smoke and kitchen fumes, and by the twaddle that is talked by the semi-educated and the demisemi-educated of Vienna as they let off their social steam at midday. At the Bräunerhof people talk either too loudly or too softly for my liking, and the service is either too slow or too fast. The Bräunerhof is inimical to all my daily requirements, yet this is precisely what makes it *the* archetypal Viennese coffeehouse—like the Café Hawelka, which became fashionable not so long ago but is now completely downmarket. I have always detested the typical Viennese coffeehouse, famous the world over, because I find everything about it inimical to me. Yet for many years it was at the Bräunerhof that I felt at home, despite the fact that, like the Hawelka, it was always *totally* inimical to me, just as I felt at home at the Café Museum and at the various other establishments I frequented during my years in Vienna. I have always hated the Viennese coffeehouses, but I go on visiting them. I have visited them every day, for although I have always hated them— and *because* I have always hated them—I have always suffered from the *Viennese coffeehouse disease*. I have suffered more from this disease than from any other. I frankly have to admit that I still suffer from this disease, which has proved the most intractable of all. The truth is that I have always hated the Viennese coffeehouses because in them I am always confronted with people like myself, and naturally I do not wish to be everlastingly confronted with people like myself, and certainly not in a coffeehouse, where I go to escape from myself. Yet it is here that I find myself confronted with myself and my kind. I find myself insupportable, and even more insupportable is a whole horde of writers and brooders like myself. I avoid literature whenever possible, because whenever possible I avoid myself, and so when I am in Vienna I have to forbid myself to visit the coffeehouses, or at least I have to be careful not to visit a so-called literary coffeehouse *under any circumstances whatever.* However, suffering as I do from the coffeehouse disease, I feel an unremitting compulsion to visit some literary coffeehouse or other, even though everything within me rebels against the idea. The truth is that the more deeply I detest the literary coffeehouses of Vienna, the more strongly I feel compelled to frequent them. Who knows how my life would have developed if I had not met Paul Wittgenstein at the height of the crisis that, but for him, would probably have pitched me headlong into the literary world, the most repellent of all worlds, the world of Viennese writers and their intellectual morass, for at the height of this crisis the obvious course would have been to take the easy way out, to make myself cheap and compliant, to surrender and throw in my lot with the literary fraternity. Paul preserved me from this, since he had always detested the literary coffeehouses. It was thus not without reason, but more or less to save myself, that from one day to the next I stopped frequenting the so-called literary coffeehouses and started going to the Sacher with him—no longer to the Hawelka but to the Ambassador, etc., until eventually the moment came when I could once more *permit* myself to go to the literary coffeehouses, when they no longer had such a deadly effect on me. For the truth is that the literary coffeehouses do have a deadly effect on a writer. Yet it is equally true that I am still more at home in my Viennese coffeehouses than I am in my own house at Nathal. I am more at home in Vienna generally than I am in Upper Austria, which I prescribed for myself as a survival therapy sixteen years ago, though I have never been able to regard it as my *home*. This is no doubt because right from the beginning I isolated myself far too much in Nathal and not only did nothing to counter this isolation but actually promoted it, consciously or unconsciously, to the point of utter despair. After all, I have always been a townsman, a city dweller, and the fact that I spent my earliest childhood in Rotterdam, Europe's biggest seaport, has always had an important influence on my life; it is therefore not without reason that once I am in Vienna, I find that I can breathe freely again. On the other hand, after a few days in Vienna I have to flee to Nathal to avoid suffocating in the loathsome Viennese air. Hence, in recent years I have made a habit of switching between Vienna and Nathal at least every other week. Every other week I flee from Nathal to Vienna and then from Vienna to Nathal, with the result that I have become a restless character who is driven back and forth between Vienna and Nathal in order to survive, whose very existence depends on this strictly imposed rhythm—coming to Nathal to recover from Vienna, and going to Vienna to recuperate from Nathal. This restlessness is inherited from my maternal grandfather, who was forced to spend his whole life in just such a state of nerve-wearing restlessness, which in the end destroyed him. All my forebears were afflicted by the same restlessness and could never bear to stay in one place for long. Three days in Vienna and I have had enough—three days in Nathal and I have had enough. In the last years of his life my friend adopted the same rhythm and often accompanied me to Nathal and back. Once in Nathal I ask myself what I am doing here, and I ask myself the same question when I arrive in Vienna. Basically, like nine tenths of humanity, I always want to be somewhere else, in the place I have just fled from. In recent years this condition has, if anything, become worse: I go to and from Vienna at diminishing intervals, and from Nathal I will often go to some other big city, to Venice or Rome and back, or to Prague and back. The truth is that I am happy *only when I am sitting in the car*, between the place I have just left and the place I am driving to. I am happy only when I am traveling; when I arrive, no matter where, I am suddenly the unhappiest person imaginable. Basically I am one of those people who cannot bear to be anywhere and are happy only between places. Years ago I believed that such a fatal condition would soon lead inevitably to total madness, which I have dreaded all my life, but in fact it preserved me from it. My friend Paul suffered from the same disease: for many years he was always traveling, simply in order to get away from one place and go to another, but he never succeeded in finding happiness on arrival. This was something we often talked about. In the first half of his life he traveled back and forth between Paris and Vienna, between Madrid and Vienna, and between London and

Vienna, as was normal for someone of his background and means. I did the same—naturally on a more modest scale, though no less obsessively—switching between Nathal and Vienna, between Venice and Vienna, even between Rome and Vienna. I am the happiest traveler—when I am on the move, moving on or moving off—but the unhappiest arriver. Clearly this is a morbid condition. We shared another obsession, which can also be classified as a disease. This is the *counting disease*, from which Bruckner also suffered in his latter years. For whole weeks and months I have a compulsion, whenever I take a streetcar into the city, to look out of the window and count the spaces between the windows of the buildings along the route, or the windows themselves, or the doors, or the spaces between the doors; the faster the streetcar travels, the faster I have to count, and I feel I have to go on counting until I am almost demented. Thus, when traveling by streetcar through Vienna or some other city, I have often tried to escape this counting sickness by making a point of not looking out of the window and fixing my eyes on the floor, but this requires tremendous self-control, of which I am not always capable. My friend Paul also had this counting disease, but to a far more serious extent, and he often told me that it made traveling by streetcar unendurable. And we shared another habit that often drives me to distraction: when walking along the sidewalk he would not, like other people, step on the paving stones indiscriminately but had to proceed according to a carefully thought-out system: for instance, after two whole paving stones he had to place his foot precisely at either the top or the bottom end of the third, not indiscriminately in the middle. With people like us nothing could be left to chance or carelessness—everything had to be thought out with geometrical, symmetrical, and mathematical precision. I observed Paul's counting disease and his eccentric walking habits *right from the beginning*. People always talk about the attraction of opposites, but in our case the attraction was due to the countless things we had in common; this soon struck me about him, and him about me. We shared so many hundreds and thousands of likes and dislikes, often being attracted to the same people and repelled by the same people. But this does not mean that we agreed about everything, that all our tastes and opinions were identical. He loved Madrid, for instance—I hated it. I loved the Adriatic—he hated it; and so on. However, we both loved Schopenhauer, as well as Novalis and Pascal, Velázquez and Goya, and we were both equally repelled by the wild but utterly unartistic El Greco. In the last months of his life, the *Herr Baron* was a mere shadow of his former self, as they say, and the more spectral the shadow became, the more everyone dissociated himself from it. I myself could naturally not feel the same about Paul's shadow as I had felt about the real Paul of earlier days. We hardly saw each other, because he often did not leave his apartment in the Stallburggasse for days on end, and we seldom arranged to meet. The *Herr Baron was going out like a light*, as they say. From time to time, without his suspecting it, I saw him in the city center, walking along laboriously, yet trying hard to maintain his accustomed bearing, by the walls of the houses in the Graben, into the Kohlmarkt and up to St. Michael's Church, then into the Stallburggasse. He was only the shadow of a man, in a very real sense, and this shadow suddenly frightened me. I did not dare to go up and speak to him. I preferred to have a bad conscience rather than to meet him. As I watched him, I suppressed my conscience and refrained from approaching him, because I was suddenly afraid. We shun those who bear the mark of death, and this is a form of baseness to which even I succumbed. Quite deliberately, out of a base instinct for self-preservation, I shunned my friend in the last months of his life, and for this I cannot forgive myself. Seen from across the street, he was like someone to whom the world had long since given notice to quit but who was compelled to stay in it, no longer belonging to it but unable to leave it. Dangling from his emaciated arms—*grotesque, grotesque*—were the shopping nets in which he laboriously carried home his purchases of fruit and vegetables, naturally apprehensive that someone might see him in this wretched state and afraid of what they might think. Perhaps the reason I did not go up and speak to him was that I was equally embarrassed and wished to spare him. I do not know whether it was because I was afraid of someone who was the embodiment of death or because I felt I had to spare him an encounter with someone who was not yet destined to go the same way. It was probably both. Watching him, I felt ashamed. I felt it shameful that I was not yet finished, as my friend already was. I am not a good character. I am quite simply not a good person. I dissociated myself from my friend, like all the others who had been his friends, because, like them, I wanted to dissociate myself from death and was afraid of being brought face to face with it. For *everything* about my friend now spoke of death. Toward the end he naturally did not try to make contact. *I* had to get in touch with him, but I did so at longer and longer intervals, constantly inventing new and more pathetic excuses. Now and then we went to the Sacher and the Ambassador, and of course to the Bräunerhof, which was the most convenient meeting place for him. When I could not get out of it I met him alone, but I preferred to go with friends, so that they could share the dreadful burden, which was almost too much to bear alone. The more remorseless his disintegration, the more elegantly he dressed, but the expensive and elegant clothes he wore—inherited from a Prince Schwarzenberg who had died years earlier—made the sight of him sheer torture, for there was scarcely any life left in him. The sight was not grotesque but simply shocking. No one really wanted to have anything more to do with him, for the person they occasionally saw in the city center, carrying his shopping nets or standing utterly exhausted by the wall of some building, was no longer the man to whom they had been attracted for years, who had entertained and endured them, whose endless cosmopolitan fooleries had relieved their mindless boredom and whose jokes and anecdotes had given them something that they, in their Viennese and Upper Austrian stolidity, could never match. Gone were the days when he would give absurd accounts of his worldwide travels or when he would indulge his fondness for irony and sarcasm and deploy all his theatrical talents in merciless accounts of his family, whose contempt had hardened into hatred and whom he described as a curiosity cabinet containing a collection of Catholic-Jewish-Nazi specimens. Nothing he now had to offer had the whiff of the big wide world, as they say; there was only the odor of wretchedness and death. His clothes, though as elegant as ever, no longer made the same debonair impression or aroused the same unfailing admiration: they seemed shabby and threadbare, like anything he still ventured to say. He no longer took taxis to Paris, or even to Traunkirchen or Nathal, but sat huddled in the corner of a second-class compartment on his way to Gmunden or Traunkirchen, wearing woolen socks and carrying a plastic bag containing his tennis shoes, which were now his favorite footwear. On his last visit to Nathal he wore a dirty postwar polo shirt, which was made for him in the days when he was a sailing enthusiast and had been out of fashion for nearly half a century, and the tennis shoes I have just mentioned. On entering the yard he no longer looked up but stared fixedly at the ground. Even the most delightful music I played him, a Bohemian wind quartet, only briefly dispelled his despondency. Various names cropped up, names of lifelong companions who had long since withdrawn their companionship. But no proper conversation developed. He spoke in disjointed, incoherent phrases. Most of the time, when he thought he was unobserved, his mouth hung open, and his hands trembled. As I drove him back to Traunkirchen, to what he called his hill, he sat silently clutching his plastic bag, which contained a few apples that he had collected in my garden. During this journey I recalled his behavior at the first performance of my play *The Hunting Party*, an unprecedented flop for which the Burgtheater provided all the requisite conditions. The absolutely third-rate actors who performed in the play did not give it a chance, as I was soon forced to recognize, in the first place because they did not understand it and in the second because they had a low opinion of it, but being a makeshift cast assembled at short notice, they had no option but to act in it. They could not be blamed even indirectly, after the failure of the original plan to assign the principal roles to Paula Wessely and Bruno Ganz, for whom I had written the play. In the event, neither appeared in it because the whole ensemble of the *Burg* (as the Viennese call it, with a kind of perverse affection) joined forces to prevent Bruno Ganz from appearing at the Burgtheater. Their opposition was prompted not only by existential *dread*, as it were, but by existential *envy*, for Bruno Ganz, a towering theatrical genius and the greatest actor Switzerland has ever produced, inspired the ensemble with what I would describe as the *fear of artistic death*. It still strikes me as a sad and sickening piece of perversity, and an episode in Viennese theater history too disgraceful to be lived down, that the actors of the Burgtheater should have attempted to prevent the appearance of Bruno Ganz, going so far as to draw up a written resolution and threaten the management, and that the attempt should have actually succeeded. For as long as the Viennese theater has existed, decisions have been made not by the theater director but by the actors. The theater director has no say, least of all at the Burgtheater, where all the decisions are made by the *matinee idols*, who can be unhesitatingly described as feebleminded—on the one hand because they have no understanding of the theatrical art and on the other hand because they quite brazenly prostitute the theater, both to its own detriment and to that of the public—though it has to be added that for decades, if not for centuries, the public has been prepared to put up with these Burgtheater prostitutes and allowed them to dish up the worst theater in the world. When once these *matinee idols*, with their celebrated names and feeble theatrical intelligence, are raised to their pedestals by the mindless theatergoing public, they maintain themselves at the pinnacle of their artistic inanity by totally neglecting whatever theatrical potential they possess and shamelessly exploiting their popularity, and stay on at the Burgtheater for decades, usually until they die. After the appearance of Bruno Ganz had been prevented by the machinations of his colleagues, Paula Wessely, my first and only choice for the role of the general's wife in the play, also withdrew. Thus, having foolishly entered into a binding contract with the Burgtheater, I had to put up with a first performance that I can only describe as unappetizing and that, as I have indicated, was *not even well intentioned*. For, faced with the least displeasure on the part of the audience, the totally untalented actors who were cast in the main parts at once took sides with the audience, following the age-old tradition by which Viennese actors conspire with the audience against a play and have no compunction about stabbing the author in the back as soon as they sense that the audience does not take to his play in the first few minutes, because it does not understand it and finds both the author and the play too difficult. It goes without saying, of course, that actors ought to go through fire, as they say, for an author and his play, especially if it is new and has not been tried out before, but unlike their colleagues in the rest of Europe, Viennese actors—and especially those at the Burgtheater—are not prepared to do this. If they sense that the audience is not instantly enthusiastic about what it sees and hears after the curtain goes up, they at once desert the author and his play and make common cause with the audience, prostituting themselves and turning what it pleases them, in their infantile presumption, to call *the premier stage of German-speaking Europe* into the world's first theatrical whorehouse. And the disastrous opening of my *Hunting Party* was not the only occasion on which they have done this. I could see from my seat in the first gallery that these Burgtheater actors turned against me and my play as soon as the curtain went up, because it did not instantly catch on, as they say. They immediately trimmed their acting accordingly and gave an atrocious performance of the first act, as though they were in duty bound to play my *Hunting Party* in such a way as to say to the audience, *We're against this frightful, inferior, revolting play*, not the management, who've *forced* us to perform it. We're performing it, but we'd rather have nothing to do with it; we're performing it, but it's worthless; we're performing it, but only with reluctance. In no time they had allied themselves with the audience and killed me and my play stone dead, as they say, betraying my producer and delivering the most insolent *coup de grâce* to my *Hunting Party*. Naturally the play I had written was quite different from the one that was actually performed by these unspeakably perfidious thespians. I could scarcely bear to sit through the first act, and as soon as the curtain came down I jumped up and left, conscious of having been deliberately and monstrously betrayed. It was clear after the first few sentences that the actors were against me and were going to wreck my play. In the first few minutes they made it a vehicle for their

artistic indigence and their opportunistic toadying to the
audience, betraying me and making my play ridiculous
when they should have been passionately committed to
bringing it safely into the world. Leaving the gallery, I
ran to the cloakroom, where the woman in charge said,
You don't like it either, sir, right? Furious with myself for
perversely allowing my play to be produced at the Burgtheater and for signing such a foolish contract, I ran down
the staircase and out of the theater. I could not have stayed
a moment longer. I remember running from the theater
as if I were running away from an institution that had
destroyed not only my play but my whole mental capacity.
I ran round the whole of the Ring and into the inner city,
and was naturally unable to calm myself down by running
backward and forward like this in my fury. Afterward I
met several friends who had attended the performance.
They all averred that it had been *a great success* (these were
their very words) and that at the end there had been
tremendous applause. They were lying. I have always had
an infallible instinct, and I knew that it could only have
been a disaster. *A great success, tremendous applause*, they
went on saying, even after we had taken our places at the
restaurant. I could have slapped their faces for their
mendacity. They even went so far as to praise the actors—
the most stupid and untalented actors ever, who had played
the gravediggers to my *Hunting Party*. The only one who
told me the truth was my friend Paul. He called the whole
performance a total misunderstanding, an utter disaster, a
typical example of Viennese cultural insolence, a classic
instance of the viciousness of the Burgtheater toward an
author and his play. *You too have become a victim of the*

imbecility and intrigues and underhand dealings that go on at the Burgtheater, he said. *It doesn't surprise me. Let it be a lesson to you.* We naturally despise people who lie to us and respect those who tell us the truth. It therefore went without saying that I respected Paul. The dying draw in their heads and want nothing to do with the living, with those who have no thought of dying. Paul had completely withdrawn from the world. He was no longer to be seen, though people occasionally asked after him. Our mutual friends asked me what Paul was doing, and I asked them. Like them, I no longer had the courage to visit him in his apartment. Sitting alone at the Bräunerhof, beneath his apartment, as I had done for some time, drinking my coffee next to his empty place and looking out into the Stallburggasse, I suddenly hated the Bräunerhof, not only because Paul was not there but because I was still going there, without him. I reflected that in my whole life I had possibly never had a better friend than the one who was compelled to lie in bed, probably in a pitiful condition, in the apartment above me, and whom I no longer visited because I was afraid of a *direct* confrontation with death. I constantly repressed this thought and finally expelled it from my mind. I confined myself to searching through my notes, some of which, as I now see, go back more than twelve years, for those passages that related to Paul, trying to visualize him as the man I wanted to remember, the *living man, not the dead*. But I now realized that these notes, which I had made in Nathal and Vienna, in Rome and Lisbon, in Zurich and Venice, were the record of a man's dying. I had met Paul, as I now see, precisely at the time when he was obviously beginning to die, and, as these notes testify, I had *traced* his dying over a period of more than twelve years. And I had used Paul's dying for my own advantage, exploiting it for all I was worth. It seems to me that I was basically nothing but the twelve-year witness of his dying, who drew from his friend's dying much of the strength he needed for his own survival. It is not farfetched to say that this friend had to die in order to make my life more bearable and even, for long periods, possible. Most of the notes I made about Paul relate to music and crime, to the Hermann Pavilion and the Ludwig Pavilion and the intense relations between the two, to the Wilhelminenberg, our hill of destiny, and to the doctors and patients who peopled it in 1967. However, he also had some remarkable things to say about politics, about wealth and poverty, all on the basis of his own experience, the experience of one of the most sensitive men I have known. He despised the society of today, which resolutely denies its own history and which consequently, as he once put it, has *neither a past nor a future* and has succumbed to the mindlessness of *atomic science*. He castigated our *corrupt government* and our *megalomaniac parliament*, as well as the vanity that had gone to the heads of artists, especially the so-called *performing* artists. He called the government, parliament, and the whole nation into question, as well as the creative and the so-called interpretative arts, just as he constantly called himself into question. He both loved and hated nature, just as he loved and hated art, and he loved and hated human beings with equal passion and equal ruthlessness. As a rich man he saw through the rich, and as a poor man he saw through the poor; as a sick man he saw through the sick, and as a healthy man he saw through the healthy; and, finally, as a madman he saw through the mad. One last time, shortly before his death, he made himself the central figure of his own legend, the groundwork of which had been laid decades before by himself and his friends. Armed with a loaded revolver, he went into Köchert's the jewelers, whose premises in the Neuer Markt had once been his parents' house and which were owned (and still are) by his cousin Gottfried. Standing in the doorway, he is reported to have threatened to shoot his cousin on the spot unless he handed over *a certain pearl*. His cousin, who was standing behind a showcase, is reported to have put up his hands in mortal terror, whereupon my friend said, *The pearl from your crown!* It was all a joke. It was to be Paul's last. The jeweler failed to understand the joke, but he realized instantly that his cousin Paul was once again *not responsible for his actions*, as they say, and ought to be in an institution. It is reported that he managed to grapple with the madman and call the police, who took Paul away to Steinhof. *Two hundred friends will come to my funeral and you must make a speech at the graveside*, Paul once told me. But I know that only eight or nine people attended his funeral. I was in Crete at the time, writing a play, which I destroyed as soon as it was finished. I learned later that he died just a few days after the *assault* on his cousin, though curiously not, as I at first believed, in Steinhof—his *real* home, as he called it—but in a hospital in Linz. He lies, as they say, in the Central Cemetery in Vienna. To this day I have not visited his grave.

A NOTE ABOUT THE AUTHOR

THOMAS BERNHARD was born in 1931 and grew up in Salzburg and in Vienna, where he studied music. In 1957 he began a second career, as a playwright, poet, and novelist. The winner of the three most distinguished and coveted literary prizes awarded in Germany, he has become one of the most widely translated and admired writers of his generation. His novels already published in English include *Gargoyles*, *The Lime Works*, *Correction*, *Concrete*, and *Woodcutters*; a number of his plays have been produced off Broadway, at the Tyrone Guthrie Theatre in Minneapolis, and at theaters in London and throughout Europe. The five segments of his memoir were published in one volume, *Gathering Evidence*, in 1985. Mr. Bernhard lives in Upper Austria.

A NOTE ON THE TYPE

THIS BOOK WAS SET in a modern adaptation of Caslon Old Face No. 2, designed by William Caslon (1692–1766). The first of a famous English family of type designers and founders, he was originally an apprentice to an engraver of gunlocks and gun barrels in London. In 1716 he opened his own shop, for silver chasing and making bookbinders' stamps. The printers John Watts and William Bowyer, admirers of his skill in cutting ornaments and letters, advanced him money to equip himself for type founding, which he began in 1720.

In style Caslon was a reversion to earlier type styles. Its characteristics are remarkable regularity and symmetry, and beauty in the shape and proportion of the letters; its general effect is clear and open but not weak or delicate. For uniformity, clearness, and readability it has perhaps never been surpassed.

Composed by Penn Set, Bloomsburg, Pennsylvania
Printed and bound by R. R. Donnelley & Sons,
Harrisonburg, Virginia
Designed by Virginia Tan